The Art of the
Shmooze

Bret Saxon & Steve Stein

S.P.i.
BOOKS

For further information, contact:

S.P.I. Books
136 West 22nd Street
New York, NY 10011
Tel: 212/633-2023
FAX: 212/633-2123

9 8 7 6 5 4 3 2
First Edition

Library of Congress Cataloging-in-Publication Data available.

S.P.I. Books World Wide Web address: spibooks.com

Printed in Canada

ISBN: 1-56171-976-5

Jacket designed by Paul Perlow Design

Photographs © 1997, 1998 courtesy of the Saxon—Stein Collection

Illustrations © 1998 by Bret Saxon

Use this book for good,

not evil...

-Bret Saxon

-Steve Stein

Contents

The Art of the

Shmooze

1

INTRODUCTION

Shmooze. Try to explain the word's meaning and we are certain you will find it difficult to define. Networking? Connecting? Bonding? Improving relationships? Establishing rapport? Yes, it is all these things—and more.

Some would characterize it as "chit chat"—light fluffy conversation that lacks any actual substance. Others would consider this practice to be a little more sinister—"to kiss up to someone."

But none of these definitions truly encapsulates the full meaning of Shmooze. A better explanation lies somewhere in the practitioner's gut and mind. A salesman can believe that he is the master Shmoozer as he exclaims to a potential customer,

"BUT WAIT! There's more! If you buy now I'll throw in this set of Ginsu knives!" Or, a corporate ladder-climber might think he is effectively Shmoozing when he tells the boss how nice her new hairstyle looks.

Yes, these are versions of Shmoozing. But Shmoozing can be found everywhere: talking your way out of a parking ticket, meeting potential dating partners, trying to sell something, socializing at parties, attempting to persuade someone, and even in closing an important business deal. These are all varieties of Shmoozing. But until you are aware of all the subtleties behind Shmoozing—until you put all the pieces together and understand the "Art of the Shmooze", you are merely using elementary Shmoozing techniques—amateur Shmoozing, if you will.

This book will take you above and beyond the obvious basics. Our approach will teach you to be a true master of the Shmooze. We will also help you to understand the real definition of Shmoozing: the intelligent, savvy use of all your social and business skills, from conversation to etiquette to strategizing—for the purpose of ultimately getting what you want.

My name is Bret Saxon. In this book, my partner Steve Stein and I will show you the ropes to high level Shmoozing. We'll give you guided step-by-step lessons in the art of the Shmooze, providing you with invaluable tips and techniques all along the way.

Those at the Top of Their Professions

Steve and I have spent the last fifteen years developing, fine tuning and mastering our Shmoozing techniques for use in one of our favorite hobbies—meeting and socializing with those at the top of their profession. We found it imperative to learn how to Shmooze effectively, in order to establish meaningful conversations with celebrities and the power elite that always surround them. We had to master the art of the Shmooze in order to be taken seriously and to impress upon whoever we are dealing with that we were deserving of their time and attention.

Those at the top of their professions are accustomed to dozens of strangers approaching them each and every day. If Steve and I merely ran up to a famous individual or a celebrity and started gushing "We loved your last movie!" or "We read about your last big deal!", we would be guaranteed not to be taken seriously and we would get politely brushed aside. Therefore, we recognized it was essential to fine-tune our conversational skills and work on our own unique techniques for meeting and talking to people who are powerful and accomplished in their professions—and we call this the Art of the Shmooze.

In order for us to stand out from the rest of the crowd, we developed these special techniques which you will now be able to study and benefit from. They not only helped us start serious conversations with famous celebrities and those at the top of their fields, but more importantly, we were able to develop lasting friendships with many of them as well.

We quickly realized that our newfound skills at Shmoozing could be useful in a variety of other situations such as, meeting new people or successfully approaching members of the opposite sex (ending up with a date or more) or improving negotiating skills or really nailing the big interview and getting that job you've always wanted.

We even went on to use our Shmoozing skills to get a major publishing deal where we wrote the bestselling book *"How to Meet and Hang Out With the Stars"* two years ago. And then we set our sights even higher and Shmoozed our way into an incredible television deal where our ideas for a humorous TV series were actually picked up by a major Hollywood television studio, Vin DiBona Productions—the folks that bring us *"America's Funniest Home Videos"* each week!

But, signing a major international television deal was not enough—we decided to Shmooze our way into the boardroom of the TV studio to convince the powers-that-be to hire us as the stars of the show! And they actually hired us to star in the forthcoming TV show, *All Access*, which will soon appear nationwide on a major television network!

Now, we are taking our skills at Shmoozing and bringing them to the mainstream market by demonstrating to you through the advice in this book, exactly how to develop the techniques necessary to quickly master the Art of the Shmooze.

Bret and Steve with Emmys (At the Emmy Awards).

We have developed new and innovative methods for building relationships and establishing a powerful rapport with just about anyone. Unlike the fawning deference you were taught to show to higher-ups—and the usual condescending response most people receive back—there are more direct, more creative methods that you can and must use to initiate and maintain relationships with those people who are seemingly "above you."

This person you would like to meet may be traditionally unapproachable, but this book is all about the art of Shmoozing

which you should be using to your best advantage. We will explain how you should communicate and how you can be completely unintimidated in the presence of that company president,
media celebrity, millionaire entrepreneur, high-powered politician, superstar athlete or even that member of the opposite sex
you deemed too gorgeous to confidently approach.

This book will also teach you how to:

☞   Be there at the *right place* and the *right time* for informal, natural, "accidental" meetings.
            (Strategically position yourself)

☞   Demonstrate warmth, intimacy and empathy rather
than sounding like a gushing fan, ardent groupie, imitative
wannabe, or predictable "suck up".
              (Inspire a positive image)

☞   Present oneself as a valuable resource, someone the
"targeted person" would really like to exchange cards with
and see again, perhaps even on a regular basis.
              (Create a valuable image)

☞   Overcome fears, awkwardness and nervousness associated with first encounters with new people.
                (Be sure of yourself)

☞   Exude confidence, be self-assured, and use intelligent
opening lines or ice-breakers.
          (Be prepared before your encounter)

No matter what field of business you are in or what interest you
are cultivating, we all eventually learn the truth associated with
the cynical adage: "It's not what you know, but *who* you know."
This breakthrough book will most importantly help you with the
"who you know" because if you follow our advice, you will start
meeting dozens of new people. Some will surely be able to help
you in a variety of ways in both your business and personal life.

2

SHMOOZE BASICS

First Impressions:
Opening Lines and Confidence

To become an expert Shmoozer one must learn both *situational techniques* that will enable you to improve situations you are in, such as how to upgrade your hotel room attend a closed or sold-out event or get backstage at a concert, as well as *personal skills* that you would use almost any time you're communicating with somebody.

This chapter will explore the personal skills you can master and use to improve your communications and social effectiveness.

Every time you begin a conversation with somebody, you have the opportunity to make an impression. The impression you make will determine how the other person perceives you, both during the conversation, and later, in future interactions. This holds true whether you are meeting someone for the very first time, or you are dealing with someone with whom you have a long term relationship. For example, when coming home from work and beginning a conversation with your spouse, if you are withdrawn and low key, your spouse will begin to sense you had a bad day or are tired. You give signs to everyone you have conversations or interactions with that point to your personality and your mood. If you are in a bad mood and do not conceal it from your spouse or friends, it's no big deal as you will probably be happier tomorrow. However, if you give off these same signs and signals when meeting someone new, you will probably lose any opportunity to build a relationship and a positive image.

The First Two Minutes Are Crucial

That is why it is so important when meeting someone for the first time to be fully cognoscente of the fact that the first two minutes of your conversation are crucial. During and after those two minutes, you are being sized up and the other person develops an initial impression of whether you are worth talking to or not. You may come across as being funny, intelligent, sarcastic, boring, or with any number of other personality traits. The key is to be aware of the fact that you are being closely scrutinized and therefore, you must project the proper "best traits" based on your audience at the time. You have got to become like a chameleon—appeal to each encounter differently and strategically, according to what approach you perceive will work best. These considerations must be addressed if you want to become a savvy socializer.

Steve and I have worked very hard in this area to master the art of the "two minute drill." We approach people in power (those at the top of their professions, celebrities, the rich & famous, etc.) whenever we encounter them at the various events, benefits, parties, charity functions, etc. that we constantly are invited to attend, and our goal is often to begin some type of ongoing special relationship with them. We are not content to just say hello, get an autograph, exchange pleasantries and move on. Since celebrities are approached by the public literally everywhere they go, it is difficult to make a good enough impression to pique their curiosity and entice them to actually want to speak with you. Let's face reality, usually, they are just being polite and really want to get the darn conversation over with already so they can escape your boring, unimpressive presence!

Steve and I have fine-tuned our opening act or rap into a two minute drill and we can usually get an excellent conversation going with all of the accomplished people we choose to meet through our socializing and travels.

Bret with Arnold Schwarzenegger (At the Oscar Awards).

The Key When Approaching People At The Top

The key with people at the top and celebrities is to get them into a conversation about some non-business or show business related topic. We will do a little homework and find out about a certain famous person's hobbies or interests and strategically begin a conversation about a specific topic that we already know is dear to them.

For example, we saw Arnold Schwarzenegger at the Golden Globe Awards and he was constantly being approached by admirers. Most people were giving him the typical "I'm a huge fan" or "I loved you in *Batman and Robin*" or in *"Terminator"*. Arnold would respond with a polite, automatic "Thank you" and extricate himself from the boring conversations, as quickly as possible. When my partner and I moved in to begin our conversation with Arnold, we started off by talking about something original that we knew he would enjoy, the subject of cigars. Arnold is a huge cigar lover and he was happy to sit down with us and discuss this favorite topic of his. During our conversation, we could see people walk by us wondering, "Why is Arnold Schwarzenegger spending so much time with those two?" The answer is found in the art of the Shmooze!

You must make a good impression and make the conversation interesting. If you accomplish this, most people will actually want to talk to you. Your Shmoozing will translate into the perception by the people who have spoken with you, that you are interesting and you have a great personality.

Let's take a step-by-step look at just how this is done.

Project Confidence

In the overall scheme of things, nothing is more important in the world of Shmoozing than projecting confidence. Are you afraid to talk in front of groups? Are you normally shy when meeting new people? Get over it. It is almost just that simple.

This book will give you hundreds of techniques to use in your quest to become comfortable in conversations, and your knowledge of all of these tips will practically force you to become more confident. But you do not need to rely solely on these suggested techniques for added confidence.

If you are shy about using these approaches, practice setting small goals for yourself that are easily accomplishable. Even if the goals seem excessively simplistic (talk a waitress into substituting mashed potatoes for the green beans, or talk the worker at the movie snack bar into giving you an extra cup of ice for your drink). Once you begin to see that talking to people and persuading them to do what you want is no big deal, and that you can accomplish what you set out to do, you will begin building confidence for bigger social tasks. Tell yourself that whatever situation you are getting yourself into, it is no big deal. You can handle it. You will succeed. You will come out on top. More times than not, this sort of thinking will turn into a self-fulfilling prophecy. If you are sure of yourself, you will carry yourself in such a way as to be successful. If you are nervous or shy, or in a bad mood, you are setting yourself up for unnecessary failure. So, if you are feeling nervous or shy, the solution is to practice covering up those feelings and that outward appearance and begin acting as if you are happy, confident and sure of yourself. Unfortunately, perception is everything. Remember, in the world of savvy socializing, **_You don't get a second chance to make a good first impression!_**

So, the successful Shmooze begins with confidence. Confidence that you can do what you set out to do, that you can talk to, and impress, anyone you choose, that you can accomplish your goals in a particular Shmoozing situation. With this self-assurance, it is time to move on to an actual encounter.

The Importance of Opening Lines

When you walk up to someone and introduce yourself or are introduced by someone else, your opening Shmoozing line soon follows. Make it good. An opening line can go a long way toward creating that impression that you are worth talking to. A bad opening line will not always be the kiss of death, but it is certainly easier and wiser to start out on a good footing. We would like to emphasize what we stated before, ***You never get a second chance to make that good first impression!***

A good opening line that Steve and I used recently, and that we'd like to share with you, was when we met Robert DeNiro at the Director's Guild for a major movie premier. We watched dozens of people approach Mr. DeNiro, each getting shot down with a polite smile, handshake and then a leave-me-alone look, or, worse yet with DeNiro's hasty escape and disappearance to another side of the room. We knew we had to be interesting quickly, if we were to avoid the same fate. Knowing that he is a big fan of sushi, when we approached him I shrewdly said, "My aunt is flying into LA tomorrow. Can you recommend any good sushi restaurants?"

Not that overly creative, but my opening line definitely worked, as DeNiro smiled and began listing restaurants and telling us what specialty he recommended she order at each place. We were able to talk with the famous actor for about twenty

Bret with Warren Beatty (At the Golden Globe Awards).

minutes that night, all because of a good opening line. And the benefits did not stop there. DeNiro actually took the trouble to introduce us to Warren Beatty, another celebrity who does not put up with gushing fans and is typically impossible to get a conversation going with. Naturally, we successfully Shmoozed along with Warren as well and had quite a memorable night!

As explained, the keys to standing out from the rest of the pack when talking with famous people and celebrities is to discuss something they have interest in and to make sure it is non-business related. You should note that this advice can work equally well for you in other social situations.

When you are meeting new people, it always helps to be interested in their interests. You can save your preferences and hobbies for another time, once you no longer have to be concerned about the positive first impression stage of your relationship.

It is also wise to play up any mutual experiences. If you are meeting new people or out on a first date and you find out that your new love interest is from Kalamazoo, tell him or her about your experiences in Kalamazoo. It does not matter if your entire connection is that your great-grandmother's nephew knew a girl in Kalamazoo, or if you were diverted there for two hours on a flight to Chicago. Any connection will create a positive moment, and that is the way you start effectively Shmoozing people. Keep trying to create those positive moments. Remember, make it fun to be with you and your targeted person will want to make sure that they can soon repeat the experience.

If your opening line backfires in some way, pick yourself up and keep on trying. It's not the end of the world. Steve and I recently met Jim Belushi at a cigar convention in Orlando. Steve opened with a joke, "Jim, I hear you turned down a role in the new *Blues Brothers* movie. They offered you 20 million and you wanted 22 million!"

Jim not only didn't think this was funny, he did not realize it was a joke and shot angrily back at Steve, "That's bullshit. Who's the ass who told you that?"

Whoops! Steve immediately realized he was bombing and quickly told him he was only joking, but Jim shook his head in

Steve Shmoozing with Antonio Banderas and Melanie Griffith (At a private party in Orlando).

disgust and made some caustic remarks about comedians who are just not funny. Let me assure you, at that moment in time, things could not have been going much worse for us. We blew it in a big way. But we are Shmoozers and we believe that no social situation is ever completely ruined and there is always a chance to redeem yourself. Steve followed up his ineffective opening remarks with some very strong come-back conversation about Belushi's new cigar line "Loan Wolf" and Jim then quickly loosened up. An hour later, we parted company after Jim Belushi had invited us to a private party later that night. We showed up to the party where we met a wealth of stars including, Antonio Bandaras and Melanie Griffith. We managed to turn around an ugly situation we had accidentally created by using the tried–and–true technique of talking about something we knew the celeb really was into.

Now we will go over some important pointers for creating positive first impressions. Practice these and you're half-way there to becoming a savvy socializer.

Eye Contact

It may seem obvious, but eye contact is supremely important in new encounters. When you are in a conversation with someone and they are constantly looking around monitoring the room, you get the feeling that they would probably like to be somewhere else instead of there talking to you. Be sure not to do this in your conversations with new people.

Or if the person you are speaking with is awkwardly looking down, or away from you, one gets the feeling that they are shy or nervous or feeling guilty in some way. Be sure also not to convey these feelings to the new person you are talking to.

Shmoozing Don'ts

All of these nervous traits will hurt your Shmoozing goals. Do not be fidgety with your eyes. Maintain your eye contact. This demonstrates confidence, sincerity, seriousness and a host of other positive things. When you are looking right at the person who is speaking, they feel you are giving them your undivided attention and that you are truly interested in what they are saying. The better you master this technique, the more you will

Steve with Teri Hatcher (At an L.A. celebrity fundraiser at Chasen's Restaurant).

notice that your conversation partner becomes excited about their topic, and excited about talking to you. Good eye contact can easily create another positive moment and then you are back on your way to building your good first impression.

A couple of years ago, Steve and I met Teri Hatcher. When introduced to someone new, we noticed that often she would stare into their eyes until they ended the eye contact. We observed her use this "Deep look in the eyes" technique which would last for several minutes. It gives you quite a feeling, being stared at so intently by someone you admire. She makes a huge impression on people with that move, and it is all based on her practiced eye contact. You do not need to be so intense, but during conversations, give the speaker your full attention and always maintain the eye contact. You will be amazed at the results you can generate with this powerful weapon in your Shmoozing arsenal.

Small Talk

Small talk is another important tool in your Shmooze inventory. You do not have to solve the world's problems in every conversation. In fact, a better tact is generally to keep it light and keep it fun. Many people have trouble engaging in small talk—they either perceive it as a waste of time, superficial, or just difficult. A more accurate analysis is that small talk has the underlying power of creating and nurturing the relationship you are attempting to build. Corny, overused, uninteresting lines about "How hot the weather is!" or "So, how's the family?" can actually serve their purpose, which is to keep the conversation going. Once the conversation slows down or stops, your targeted person is likely to use the lull as an excuse to move on and ditch you. You obviously want them to stay right where they are until they recognize what a good guy or gal you are and until your positive first impression is solidly made. That is why a little small talk is good to have in your Shmooze repertoire.

You can practice small talk with your friends or family by trying to keep a conversation going as long as possible with them. Be aware that your goal is to practice small talk, so avoid personal issues that you are both already comfortable discussing. Once you master the art of transitioning a conversation using small talk with new acquaintances, your practice will pay off huge dividends as you will always be capable of moving along slow conversations that otherwise might end prematurely, thereby denying you the time you need to make your great first impression.

When you find yourself in the middle of a slow conversation, an important trick to get things interesting is to build on whatever topic your conversational partner has brought up. You might be dying to talk about the latest New York Yankee victory, but try keeping the conversation revolving around their topics if you want to charm, influence or otherwise create a positive moment. You'll find your Shmooze target much more interested in the conversation if it revolves around their preferred subjects. Keep in mind that the goal here is to build a relationship and leave your target with a positive impression of you, not for you to show your brilliance about your favorite subjects that they may care little about. Remember to always be unselfish. Work hard to ensure that whoever you are talking to enjoys the conversation. What is said is not nearly as important as the residual impression you leave them with. Be a conversational giver. Be a wise and unselfish conversationalist. And watch yourself become an expert Shmoozer!

My co-writer, Steve, was recently in a conversation with Kevin Costner at a celebrity fund raiser earlier this year and was dying to ask Kevin about *Bull Durham*, one of Steve's favorite films. But keeping in mind his goal of developing a positive first impression and, hopefully, an ongoing relationship, Steve kept shrewdly guiding the conversation back to Kevin's interests. Steve spent fifteen minutes talking with Costner about golf—one of Kevin's passions—even though Steve has never played the game, knows very little about it, and could not care less about discussing it. But Steve was Shmoozing. He did his best to make sure that his target, Kevin, was interested in their conversation topics and his efforts paid off—Steve and I were invited by Kevin to join him at his table that evening for dinner!

Steve with Kevin Costner (At a celebrity fundraiser at the Beverly Hilton).

Introductions

Life is just a little bit easier for you if you manage to get introduced to your target than if you have to go up cold and break into a conversation yourself. The problem generally is finding someone you know who also knows your intended target.

Steve and I recognized that there is a way around this little roadblock. We just walk up to people we do not know and take it upon ourselves to introduce each other. For example, at a recent Friar's Club function, Jim Carrey was in the middle of a

Bret with Jim Carrey (At The golden Globe Awards).

conversation with three other people. I could have walked up and interrupted the conversation, introduced myself, and then with everyone wondering who this bumbling, loser guy was, I could have tried to spit out some brilliant opening line. Instead, Steve and I walked up to the group and as we approached (and after catching the comedian's eye), I said to Carrey with a big smile on my face, "Jim, I wanted to introduce an associate of mine, Steve Stein. Steve this is my friend, Jim Carrey."

Now, since I did not have a previous relationship with Carrey, one might imagine that this bold move could have been very awkward for me. Wrong! Because I have the proper mental outlook, it was not awkward for me, and it never has to be awkward for you either! Using what we call the good old "pretend friend introduction," Jim immediately reacted positively and shook hands with Steve and gave him a courtesy "Nice to meet you." Now we were somewhat legitimately in the conversation with Jim Carrey and the two others and we were able to build from there. We brought up the subject of Canada, where we knew Jim was from, and broke through the crucial first impression and initial meeting phase. We ended up talking (Shmoozing it up) with Jim for a good forty-five minutes.

Of course, if you can get a legitimate introduction to a targeted person, it is that much better. But an introduction from a "pretend friend" has almost never failed for us. This technique works equally well when meeting date prospects at a club, bar or disco. I have introduced dozens of friends to people in clubs whom I have never previously met. Once I make the introduction, I step back and my friend is off and running—with someone they would probably have never approached on their own. If worst comes to worst, any bad feelings are projected at the "ass" who initiated the "pretend friend" introduction and not at the unfortunate person who was just introduced. The "ass" (me), when sensing a bad vibe, just slinks away from the scene and the person who was introduced can then sincerely apologize for his rude friend and continue Shmoozing away. The end result is we achieved our mission, broke the ice, and got the Shmooze going.

Occasionally, Shmoozing can be embarrassing, but the alternative is to stand alone in a room and pray for someone to come over and talk to you. We believe in prayer in a house of worship, but we believe in taking destiny into our own hands in a social setting! Schmoozing can make something happen for you that would never occurred if you didn't take the initiative.

Buzzwords

If at all possible, do a little homework before your next potential Shmooze function and learn the buzzwords of the industry.

There is almost no quicker way to "bond" with a new acquaintance than to have similar life experiences. When you know the buzz-words, these mutual life experiences are assumed immediately.

For example, Steve and I were recently out filming segments for our upcoming humorous television show, which is called *All Access*. When you are on-camera you quickly learn that the two most important people on the shoot are the cameraman and the makeup artist. These two determine how good you will look when your image is beamed to tens of millions of television view-ers. They can make you look awful (ask Richard Nixon about the JFK debate), or they can make you look unbelievably better than you actually do. Steve and I can use all the help we can get, so we start the Shmooze immediately when we meet the cam-eraman. We will ask him if he is using Bose lights or 3 chip cam-eras, or any other intelligent technical questions we can think of. The cameraman inevitably begins to tell us his preferences on everything from shooting locations to equipment—and we listen as intently as possible while usually having no idea at all what he is talking about. The next thing you know we have a new friend for life. For the rest of the shoot, we feel comfort-able that he is on our side and looking out for our interests. Please do not get the wrong idea that this technique is all one sided and we are insincerely getting what we want by using and taking advantage of the gullibility of our cameraman. We are not. We are simply quickening the process of getting a good working relationship going. Once this relationship is created, and it is clear that the cameraman is looking out for us, we will request him on the next shoot, and the next one after that, ensuring that a lot of business goes his way.

Shmoozing can be used to fool people and get what you want. But we'd like to reiterate that it can also be used to shorten the typical "get to know you" phase creating instant bonding.

With regard to our new television show, we do not have the luxury of having the first few scenes shot with a cameraman who is not enthusiastic about us or the job. We want to ensure that this key player in our success is motivated and cares about us from the very first shot. Our Shmoozing in this situation is meant to speed up the process and helps us in our important goal of winning people over faster.

You can use buzzwords in any conversation. If you can discreetly work them in, you give the person they are directed at the feeling that you are on the inside—that you are one of them. So, learn the buzzwords pertaining to your targeted person, and use them liberally.

Our TV Show, *All Access*

By the way, in case you are wondering what our new television show *All Access* is about, let us explain the concept. The basic premise is that two regular guys, Steve and I, host an irreverent entertainment program. Steve and I go out and meet celebrities and power players in the entertainment industry, goofing on ourselves and trying to have fun along the way. Each segment on the show is designed to make viewers laugh, while at the same time taking the home audience behind the scenes with hidden cameras.

Some of the first segments we have filmed include:

☞ ***Tootsie***: We show the viewers what a Hollywood casting call is like. We used hidden cameras to cover us as we went and tried out for a role on an upcoming sitcom for Warner Brothers. The funny part was that we have no talent, so our audition was pitifully bad. Additionally, the part was for a female, so Steve and I dressed up, a la *Tootsie*, for the tryout. Needless to say, we didn't get the part, but we did get some great on-camera reactions from the producers of the sitcom—which we used as a hilarious segment for our show.

☞ ***Can He Say That?***: We were challenged to say the words "Limburger cheese and coffee" as many times as possible during a conversation with Harrison Ford. The hard part was trying to have a normal conversation with Harrison, say the words, and not come across looking totally foolish. It is a lot more difficult than it might seem to work "Limburger cheese and coffee" multiple times into a normal conversation. We met Harrison on the set of his new movie, Ivan Reitman's *6 Days, 7 Nights*. Viewers will enjoy the segment because they are in on the joke. Every time we say the phrase "Limburger cheese and coffee", the audience understands the inside joke, while Harrison Ford has no idea what our problem is. By the end of the conversation, he asked if we had a weird fascination with cheese.

☞ *It's a Cross Between Toy Story and Apocalypse Now*: If you have a great idea for a screenplay, or have already written one—you need to set up a "pitch meeting" with the movie studios to go and "pitch" your idea. Steve and I set up pitch meetings with some of the most famous producers in Hollywood and went in and pitched them the worst movie idea ever—a computer animated love story set in the middle of the Vietnam War.

The viewer gets to see on the hidden cameras, how a pitch meeting works, while at the same time watching Steve and I get yelled at, and kicked out of some of the most important offices in Hollywood. It was an awesome scam that caught some great candid moments on camera.

☞ *I'm the Best Boy*: We got ourselves on the set of Arnold Shwarzenegger's movie *Batman and Robin* and while the secret camera was rolling, we got Arnold to explain to us some of the more esoteric jobs that are available on the set, including: Best Boy, Grip, Set Dresser, etc. Steve and I then attempted to do each job for a while. As is usual, we made fools of ourselves by doing everything wrong. It was a fun segment catching Arnold and the crew on our secret cameras.

☞ *Gas Powered Turtleneck Sweater*: We approached a slew of celebrities and with the hidden cameras rolling, we asked them, with a straight face, to invest in our new business idea. Our business and product ideas were so ridiculously idiotic and bad that the rejections and private reactions from the celebrities were terrific.

☞ *Let's Get Ready to Rumble*: Steve and I demonstrated to the TV audience how we can scam our way into the actual boxing ring, minutes before the start of the first Mike Tyson/Evander Holyfield heavyweight fight. The tough part of this challenge was getting through all of the security and into the ring—there aren't a lot of extra people allowed in there right before the fight starts. As a bonus, we got some quick hair care tips from Don King.

☞ *But It's a Nice Tux*: Steve and I made an appointment
to try out as a lounge act at a big casino in Las Vegas. When
we got up on stage with the hidden cameras rolling, we were
dressed in ridiculous powder blue tuxedos with ruffled
shirts, and bell bottom pants. We told the auditioner on
the phone that we had our own large band, but we showed
up with only a boom box. When we sang, we were unbelievably awful. We have absolutely no hidden talent in us and
we can't sing one note. The lounge manager was so upset he
yelled, screamed, cursed, and threw a drink at us, before
having security guards remove us. The video footage is
priceless.

The key to our show *All Access* is that the segments need to
have something to do with entertainment, and the opportunity
must exist for Steve and I to make fools of ourselves with the
secret cameras rolling. We are pretty good at that.

Other segments on the show give viewers a behind-the-scenes
look at non-traditional celebrity events such as celebrity golf tour-
naments, softball games, dinner roasts, Vegas nights, and assorted
fund-raisers.

Bret with Steve Martin (At the golden Globe Awards).

Bret hanging out with the legendary Bill Murray (At the ESPY Awards).

The show is cutting edge—keep an eye out for it. By the way, if you have any hot ideas for interesting segments, send them to our publisher's address on the copyright page and we'll consider them for future shows.

Humor

Make them laugh, and they're yours. You can probably imagine that Steve Martin, Bill Murray or David Letterman do not have any problems Shmoozing. When you are funny and can think quickly on your feet, people love to talk with you. You become the life of the party and meeting new people and building relationships becomes that much easier.

But even if being funny does not come very naturally to you, you can still use humor to enhance your Shmoozing techniques. One method is to exploit your conversational partner's humor. When the person you are talking to makes a joke, laugh and make a point of repeating the last part of the joke or humorous story they have just related to you.

For example, if you hear a joke such as: "Do you know how to make a small fortune in book publishing? Start out with a large fortune!"

After hearing the joke, you should laugh and then repeat to the joke teller: "Start out with a large fortune!"

Don't be obvious that you are strategically using a preconceived technique. But if done correctly, you give the speaker the affirmation and good feeling that you liked their story or joke and you were really paying attention. You can also further flatter the speaker by saying to them: "Do you mind if I use that one tomorrow at work?"

Asking permission gives the story or joke teller a modest sense of power and success, and those feelings translate into another positive moment—another building block to the successful Shmooze. Obviously, if the joke or story was not that funny, do

Bret with Michael Richards (At the Grammy Awards).

not force out a phony laugh. Just force yourself to smile politely and give the speaker an understanding nod of your head. This will also serve to connect you to your targeted person, giving them the affirmation they are seeking after relating their less-than-funny joke or story to you.

Leveraging other's jokes is half the battle. But do not forget to try and be at least a little amusing and stimulating during your conversations. I do not consider myself all that funny, so you can imagine the nervousness that I feel when talking with some-one like Jay Leno or Michael Richards—who are both very funny men. But I overcome my fears by reminding myself that I am confident and successful in my Shmoozing abilities, which will enable me to open some sort of positive conversation with them.

With a little practice, you too can develop the confidence to strike up a conversation with anyone, anytime, anywhere—with-out fearing rejection. When I met with Michael Richards at an awards show recently, I played off some of his funny lines to interject some of my own humor into the conversation. My at-tempts weren't going to get me an audition as a stand-up comic, but Michael did laugh a few times when I inserted some jokes into our discussion and we did end up having a great conversa-tion. Most people want to laugh more than they want to criti-cize you, so your attempts at humor will usually be rewarded. Do not be afraid to try. It is much worse to be a dry, humor-less, boring conversationalist who will be forgotten, than to make a few jokes that do not always work so well.

You might want to avoid the pre-written setup jokes, like "Did you hear the one…", but do try to be spontaneously funny and quick-witted in the context of the conversation. Unless you are trying to create a serious image for yourself, we find it is al-ways best to keep the conversation light and lively. Use the hu-mor that is within you and try to forget you are talking with some-one who is powerful or a celebrity. Try to be playful, be natural, and have fun. Being your usual, charming self can often make you more memorable and likable than trying too hard to become what you perceive your targeted person will like.

The ability to be warm, natural and friendly is usually the greatest Schmoozing skill of all!

Current Events

When trying to Shmooze, whether out at a party or club, or at work, the conversation will often come around to some current event—be it a hot news story, sports, entertainment, or something in between. It certainly helps your chances of succeeding in your Shmooze if you are up on your current affairs stories and can "Talk the Talk". So, read the newspaper in the morning. Get familiar with as many of the top stories as you can. And study the sports section. You might not like the Dallas Cowboys, but if you know that they just won last night and you know a couple of statistics about key players, when a conversation comes around to the Cowboys during a mingle and Shmooze opportunity, you will be ready. Throw out a sports comment and you have another immediate bond—another positive moment.

There are many sources to keep abreast of current events. We read the *LA Times* every morning, and scan the *ESPN* website on the internet (www.sportszone.com), as well as the entertainment news on the *New York Post* website (The *New York Post's* gossip section known as *"Page Six"* is at www.nypostonline.com) and *the New York Daily News "Daily Dish"* by Rush & Molloy (www.mostnewyork.com).

You should also try to keep up with the local entertainment and gossip news if you are Schmoozing in another city. This will prepare you for Schmoozing even obscure, local conversations. It only takes us about fifteen minutes a day to get through all of this latest information and after this preparation we find it very rare for someone to be speaking about a piece of hot gossip or a current topic that we are not fully briefed on. If you follow this advice for two weeks, you are guaranteed to put all your friends to shame when it comes to speaking about any topic that is in the news! And your knowledge translates into power, and added confidence—which translates into you being perceived as a sharp and savvy socializer.

Bret with David Letterman (At the Emmy Awards).

At last year's Emmy Awards, David Letterman and I were discussing tuxedos when he all of a sudden asked me if I knew who won the Formula One auto race that day. I happened to have remembered hearing that Michael Schumacher, the driver for the Ferrari team, had won. I was in no way a Formula One fan, but because of this little tidbit, Dave was very thankful to me for the information and it helped prolong our interesting conversation. Dave ended up inviting Steve and I to a behind the scenes taping of his show in New York which we gratefully took him up on two months later. Trust us when we tell you that the Shmooze works!

Remember Names

Remembering names is a technique that pays huge dividends very quickly. When a waiter comes over to your table and introduces himself before he tells you about the specials, make a mental note of his name. Remember it and use it later in the evening and watch your level of service increase.

People love to know that you care enough to know their name. It may be a combination of the fact that now they are accountable (you know them and they are not just another face) and that they are truly flattered by your effort. Use people's names as often as possible. Your targeted person will always have a positive moment when you use his or her name. The more surprised they are that you know their name, the more impact it will have for you in your future dealings with that person.

Even existing relationships and friendships can benefit from the use of the "remember the name" technique. Most conversations make it all the way through without the participants mentioning each other's names. A simple "I really agree, that is a good idea, Jim", is much more powerful than if you had said the same thing and left the name out of the sentence.

Remembering someone's name a week later is also impressive and effective—it is just much more difficult. Use memory tricks to remember names like associating a person's name with a characteristic they possess. Try to incorporate a person's name into the conversation at least two or three times—especially towards the end of the conversation. For instance, by saying, "It was terrific meeting you, Beth," the personalization at the end just enhances the thought and creates that minor positive moment.

Of course, this technique does not have much effect on famous personalities or Hollywood celebrities, since they expect everyone to know their name. But often the best way to get to those who are famous is through their handlers and every handler has a name—and as we have pointed out, with every name is a Shmooze opportunity.

Repeat the Info

You are in a conversation with a new person and you recognize there is a Shmooze opportunity just waiting for you to take advantage of. It is time to go to work. Your target asks you if you happen to know Jack from Des Moines. You might have no idea who Jack is, but you reply, "Oh, sure, Jack. He's based out of Des Moines, isn't he?"

Your target will almost always miss the fact that you just repeated the very info they had just given you and they'll assume you must know Jack.

Recently, I was at the Grammy Awards speaking with two record producers. They were discussing Puff Daddy, a major recording artist, and they were telling each other "Puff" stories such as the fact that he samples a lot of his music and they had heard he can't even work his own mixing board. A few minutes later I got more active in the conversation and the topic turned back to Puff Daddy. I didn't know anything more about Puff than what I had just heard, but when it came time for me to offer my opinion, I replied, "You know, what bothers me about Puff is the fact that he is more of a management type than a creative artist. I hear he can't even work his own mixing board." The two producers whole heartedly agreed and told me I was right on the money. It never occurred to them that I had gotten my information right from their mouths minutes before. All I did was repeat the info. And bond. And effectively Shmooze. And create another important positive moment.

Nothing to Say?

You are in the middle of a conversation and someone finishes their sentence. You cannot think of any reply. You are stuck. Call it writer's block, or better yet, Shmoozer's block. You certainly don't want to let an awkward moment take over and ruin the flow of your conversation and the Shmoozing mood you have carefully worked up. So, what do you do?

After the person you're talking with is done speaking, you throw out an old standard comment with some genuine enthusiasm and a big affirming smile, such as: "There you go!" or "I hear you!" or "I know what you mean!" or "I know what you're saying!" Other lines that also usually work well are: "Exactly!" or "Fabulous!" or "Precisely!" or "I'm not arguing with you!" or "You're right on the money!"

These comments all serve to support the point the speaker just made, even if you have no idea what they were talking about. You can even throw in an occasional "Cool!", or "Right on!", although this is best said to a younger target of your Shmoozing and should obviously not be used on serious business types, your date's parents, your investors, your bosses, etc.

Taken at face value, some of these sayings don't make a lot of sense. But even if your target is talking and they say something like, "Apple Computer will be out of business within a year!" you can follow up their comment with an enthusiastic "There you go!" Despite the fact that this does not really signify anything, the comment merely reinforces in your target's mind that you were listening, you understand, and that you fully agree with his, or her, profound opinion on a subject. The person who is spending will like you a little more because you have publically agreed with them. This is basic human nature and you should keep this point in mind: people love to receive positive affirmation, especially in public.

Try using these above-mentioned lines when appropriate in your future discussions. They will become very natural for you to incorporate into your own conversational style and they will serve as easy throw-aways during conversations. Once you begin working them into your Shmooze repertoire you will wonder how you ever got along without these convenient saviors of the awkward moment.

Wrap Up

You have passed the first hurdle in becoming a master of Shmooze. These basics will hopefully give you the confidence to talk with anyone, anytime, anywhere, and enough elementary techniques to get you through 99% of your future conversations with flying colors.

Remember to relax. Remember to have fun. You hold the upper hand—because you understand the basics of the Shmooze. In the next chapter we will look at more tangible techniques that can be employed in various situations to help you with your Shmoozing.

Congratulations! You have now graduated from "Basic Shmooze".

3

HOW TO SHMOOZE
AT WORK

You can use your newfound Shmooze skills to skyrocket up the corporate ladder. Practice your personal Shmooze techniques at the office and you will find that everyone you come in contact with will find you more sociable, more fun to be with and more approachable.

Once they recognize these new traits, you will more likely be on their minds for future big projects, raises, promotions, and awards. If you can give off the perception that you are not only an efficient hard worker, but you are also very likeable, the battle is won. You can become the invaluable employee that everyone wishes they could be.

You should use all of your Shmooze techniques. Do not be shy at the office. When you include in your day-to-day personality the important Shmooze tools learned so far, such as:

- **Eye contact**
- **Using people's names**
- **Being interested in others' conversational topics**
- **Shmooze Basics from Chapter 2,**

you create an aura of good feeling everywhere you go. This translates into people at work suddenly recognizing your talent and value.

Naturally, you still have the same work skills after you begin the Shmoozing activities at the office that you had prior to your Shmoozing repertoire at work. But because your colleagues' impression of you has improved and you've discreetly created a new image for yourself, you are perceived by those around you in a vastly changed light. And perception is often what counts most in the work environment. If you've followed our advice, your office peers will enjoy working with you more and your managers will prefer to give you the new assignments—which will give you the valuable exposure you need. Savvy Shmoozing can position you to be the "go-to person" in the office. Use it to your best advantage.

Here are some specific Shmooze techniques you can use at the office:

Outside Research and Homework

Knowledge is power, and there is no reason for you to miss an opportunity to learn some of the company's future plans and directions. This is because there is an easy way for you to keep abreast of your company's needs—scan the classified ads in your newspaper every Sunday. If your company is hiring, they will probably advertise in the Sunday paper. If you see company ads you will be able to tell where in the company the hiring is taking place. This can help you identify the "hot" divisions at your firm and you can begin to plan a strategic transfer.

You can also identify new projects based on the requirements in the ads. Sometimes the ads clearly state the project being hired for, but even if the ad is not that clear, you can usually tell what project or department is in need of personnel by the listed job requirements.

While you are scanning the classified ads, also look for ads from your competitors. This will help you get a feel for the marketplace in your profession. All of this information can be useful when you are trying to get a raise, or even looking to transfer jobs. The more knowledge you have, the more power you have. Keep abreast of your surroundings and do a little homework. It can go a long way.

You should also keep in touch with customers, people from other companies in your industry, consultants, or anyone else you have had a positive business contact with. They may prove to be very valuable, down the road, if you want to change firms. These contacts will also be able to help you make a job change from a greater position of strength. Create a contact list and then schedule "keep in touch" calls. Try to call to touch base with these people once a month. The call can be short, but make it clear you are just calling to say "hi". You do not want anything, you are just keeping in touch. The last thing you want to convey is that you are trying to use them for anything. Using them for help may come later—when you are actually looking around for another job. You may even want to give them some tidbits of info you have heard or read concerning: your industry, competitors, your region, etc. This will create the impression that you are hooked in to what's happening in your field. It will also give you a reputation with those you call, that you really know what you're talking about, an impression you want to continue to nurture among your valuable contact list. The recipient of the call will be particularly flattered if they believe the call has no ulterior motive. So, Shmooze away and make sure the person you call feels at ease and comfortable with your motives.

While on the subject of research, do not forget to look around right in your own workplace. Find out what is happening in other departments within your company. This information can be very valuable to you and can identify opportunities and potential problems.

As an example, if you are a loan officer at a bank, you might ask around and see what is going on in New Accounts. If you find that they are launching a major drive to land new customers, you will know that new customers mean more money to loan. And more money to loan might mean the bank will hire an additional loan manager. With this information you can begin angling for the job before anyone else even realizes it will exist.

The opposite can also be true. If you find out the Board of Directors is looking to cut back on their risk exposure, you might recognize the negative effect this will have on your loan department down the road, and ask for a transfer—before your motives are obvious.

Another type of research that is essential for you to do is to learn how your boss perceives your work. Most people are generally reluctant to criticize, including bosses. The old saying "No news is good news" is just not true in today's workplace. If you are receiving "no news" that only means you are not trying hard enough to get the news. You should be sure to ask your boss and your colleagues for feedback on everything you do. This not only shows your genuine concern for "doing it right the first time", but it empowers and flatters those you ask because people generally love to give advice. Once you ask for the feedback/advice, a relationship begins to develop where they can become a parental figure or a mentor during these conversations. This feeling of being a mentor and guiding someone's career creates a natural relationship that occurs in most corporate environments. The mentor is more senior in the company and can provide you with invaluable advice on the strategic advancement of your career. They can also run interference for you with top management, ensuring that you get your share of good breaks and opportunities to shine. Since most people like being mentors, by developing multiple mentor relationships you will be generating additional positive moments, while at the same time receiving valuable feedback.

As a side note, we recommend that the first time you go to lunch with your boss, excuse yourself halfway through the meal and go to the cashier and pay the entire check. When your boss tries to pick up the check at the meal's end he will be very surprised and most likely impressed, as everyone else expects the boss to always pay. Your boss will compare you to every other employee he ever had lunch with who sat around waiting for him to pick up the check. This little one time maneuver successfully separates you from everyone else in the office and puts you in a completely different light in your boss's eyes. You can tell him that you will let him get the next one and make a joke out of your shrewd maneuver. Or you can tell him that you wanted to make sure you had the opportunity for a second lunch and this was the best way to make that a likely occurrence. Or you can joke that you had so much fun that you wanted to pay this time. Whatever you say, make it light and funny and be sure of yourself when you say it.

Another important thing to work on is learning your boss's impressions of your performance sooner rather than later. Do not wait for your annual review. Try to meet your boss for a quick lunch once a month—or at least schedule a meeting in the office once a month. You do not want to just walk up and ask him how you are doing, because chances are you will receive a curt automatic answer like "fine" or "okay". Once you make the subject a little more formal, through a lunch or a scheduled meeting, you will generate a lot more honesty. You may find that your project priorities are not the same as your boss's and armed with this information you can adjust before it is too late. At the very least, your boss will be impressed by your commitment to doing your job effectively and your concern for his opinion of your performance. The Shmooze continues.

Gossip Rules

When it comes to gossip, the rule is to listen and enjoy but do not fuel the fire. Many rumors turn out to be false and if you are ever heard repeating or passing along one of the false ones it can reflect very poorly on you. When someone is gossiping to you, maintain your Shmooze etiquette and appear very interested in what they are saying. Just do not add to it or pass it along.

If, in a moment of weakness, you feel that you must pass along some gossip, be very clear not to ever gossip about your boss. It is safer to gossip about co-workers since they cannot hurt you as quickly and directly. In addition, if you do say something negative about your boss, one day a jealous co-worker may repeat to your boss what you said. It's a jungle out there, so expect the worst and don't be surprised when you are back-stabbed, sold-out, or dumped—when you least expect it. Welcome to the real corporate world.

Also, be aware of the difference between put-downs and gossip. Gossip has the premise of providing some information, even if it is negative. Put-downs offer no information, just negative opinions. Steer a wide berth around put-downs. They can never help you. They only make you look petty and they can hurt you even more than gossip can, down the road.

Education

The value of education cannot be stressed enough. One thing is a constant in life and that is change. Your company will change, your job will change, the people you work with will change, and generally, everything will change. You need to be ready for the change. Try to anticipate the coming changes and prepare for them. Take some classes at the local college in finance or technology, even if it has nothing to do with your current position. The education will help position you for future assignments within the company and outside the company. More immediate than the benefit for future jobs is the impact it has on your current job. Your interest in education will always impress your

boss with your eagerness to learn. Your boss will see your edu-
cational pursuits as an attempt to raise your value to the company. This perception will certainly help you when seeking promotions and raises. You are taking actions that make you look
good in the boss's eyes which means our advice is working!

Everyone Loves a Team Player

How many job openings include in the job description "Must
be a team player", or something along those lines? A huge per-
centage of them do. If it is not spelled out in the description it
is certainly present in the mind of the person doing the hiring.
So, become a team player at your office. Do not get bogged
down with tunnel vision regarding your job and responsibilities.
See the big picture at your company and think "team work".
Have lunch with people from other departments, get to know
what is going on around you. It will only help you to perform
your job better, and it is a terrific networking opportunity. The
more people you know and who perceive you positively, the
more your perceived value to the company increases. Volunteer
to help other employees. If you volunteer you will be recognized
by those in power as a "concerned employee", "self-starter" and
most importantly, a "team player". You will also benefit from all
the other commonly expressed traits that employers are always
looking for. Create the image for yourself that you want to
project and you will be in greater control of your career.

Get a Mentor

To move through the corporate ranks, you can speed up the
process by creating a special relationship with a member of senior
management. The most obvious benefit is that they can help get you
promoted, or when they are promoted, take you up the ladder with
them. But also important is the information they can give you, such
as the current flavor of corporate politics. Your mentor can help
steer you away from potential land minds and offer advice on how
to handle certain managers that you must deal with. The information your mentor can pass along is invaluable.

You can "interview" potential mentors by inviting them to lunch and creating a new relationship. If it is awkward for you to invite someone you are interested in to lunch because they are too high up the ladder, then pick someone lower down who you do have access to and start there. If it is still awkward in your company to get a lunch meeting going, then try to get a group together for lunch. This is a less pressured situation for all involved and still allows you to interact with the person you are keen to get closer to. Perhaps after this first group lunch you will feel more comfortable setting up the one-on-one luncheon.

Occasionally you have to be blunt and express your interest in being mentored. Tell your potential mentor that you could really use someone to "show you the ropes". Some of your potential mentors might tell you they are too busy, but most people are flattered at the prospect of having a bright protégé. Hopefully, that will be you!

Be the Connection King

Develop a relationship with a travel agent and a ticket broker. It is easy to do—simply pick up the phone and talk to a couple of them and then go down to their offices and meet with the ones you liked best in person. Tell them that you will be sending business their way from your company, give them your card, and all you should ask from them in return is that they treat your referrals as if they were VIPs.

Now back at the office, let it be known that you have connections within the travel industry and the ticket world. People will start asking you if you can help with their trip to Texas or Florida, or if you can help them get tickets to the ballgame, the Rolling Stones concert or perhaps a play. You can say, "Of course I can get you those tickets", and refer them to your contacts. Call and let your contacts know you are sending someone down. When your co-worker gets to the travel agent or ticket broker, the agent will know their name, and as you had prearranged, they will treat your referrals with added care. They will also mention you as the person responsible for their special treatment. The individualized attention your co-worker will receive will make them feel special, which will translate into very positive feelings for you. You have just created another positive moment.

Miscellaneous Office Shmoozes

You can use almost all of the Shmooze techniques discussed in this book just as effectively at the office as anywhere else. But it might be valuable to point out some of the most effective office techniques.

The Top 10 Office Shmooze Techniques

Use People's Names

1. Using people's names in the office offers a huge payoff. The work environment becomes so hectic and routines become overly familiar. As a result, people use each other's names less and less in meetings and during one-on-one conversations. Sprinkle in your target's first name throughout the conversation and you will notice they gravitate towards you in future conversations. Enough cannot be said for using people's names.

Use Compliments

2. Another good rule of thumb is to pay at least four or five compliments a day. Paying a compliment requires only a couple of seconds of your time and costs you nothing, but, trust us, it will reap big payoffs by making your target feel good and giving them the impression that you care and can identify with whatever it is they are going through at the time you give them the compliments.

Be Interested In Co-Workers' Conversation

3. Another Shmooze technique that works effectively at the office is to always appear interested in having conversations with co-workers and especially with your bosses. The surest way to create a positive moment at the office is to look into their eyes and appear genuinely interested in what they have to say. During the conversation remember to be a good

listener. Do not talk too much about yourself—be interested in their subjects. Throw in your various affirmations during the conversations: quick positive nods, enthusiastic sayings such as, "There you go!" or "Exactly!" or "Precisely!" And remember the conversational Shmooze techniques covered previously. They all work wonders at the office.

Leverage Positive Feelings Toward Yourself

4. When someone is given a promotion or an award at the office, they are filled with positive feelings. Leverage those feelings towards yourself. Buy a box of doughnuts or fancy cookies and leave it on the desk of the person who got the attention, along with a congratulatory note. The gift will cost you about $4.50, but the gesture will always be remembered. You will not only get Shmooze points from the recipient, but also from the rest of the office when your gift is generously offered around to everyone.

Do Something Special For Co-Workers

5. When someone in your office has a story written about them in an industry trade magazine or company newsletter, have the story nicely framed as a gift for them. Everyone loves to have their fifteen minutes of fame and by giving them this framed story you extend their famous time. They will never forget you for it and you can create an inexpensive positive moment. Incidentally, this positive moment will be reinforced for years because the framed information will be on their wall for a long time.

Say "Thank You"

6. Remember to always say "Thank You." If someone in your office does something for you, be sure to remember to thank them. You can send them an e-mail, leave a short note on their desk, or even casually say thanks verbally. Everyone likes to feel needed and to be stroked. Everyone wants to be sure that their efforts do not go unnoticed. A little "Thank You" goes a long way.

Become Active In Company Publications

7. Get involved in the company newsletter or in-house publications. As a contributor to the newsletter, you have an excuse to go and talk with department heads all over the company. As you "interview" them for a story profile, you have a terrific opportunity to Shmooze and bond with the important people that run the whole company. The best part is that these managers are suddenly doing their best to Shmooze you so the article turns out as positive as possible for them. When the article comes out in the newsletter, you create another positive moment by giving the department heads their period of fame. If you really want to play the game, you should go out and not only write the article, but also frame the article and present it to your target.

Discretely "Gift" The Right People

8. A $1.00 Snapple can go a long way. Bring your boss's secretary a beverage or something else they like, at least once a week. Not only will you create a positive moment with her or him, but you will create a valuable ally to have in your corner. Now when a report is due to your boss by 5:00 on Friday, but you need the weekend to put it together, your boss's secretary can get you the extra time you need by turning it in on Monday as if it was on her or his desk since Friday. More importantly, secretaries can have a surprisingly large influence on the boss when it comes to positive impressions of employees and to their annual raises.

Remember Birthdays

9. Birthdays are a great opportunity to create a positive moment. Invest in a $1.49 greeting card and a couple of lottery tickets and you can give an inexpensive, but very fun, birthday gift. Create a tickler file with co-workers' birthdays and always remember them. People are very impressed and touched when you remember their birthday.

Organize A Company Event

10. Organize a company outing or event. You can organize a fun event like a company trip to the bowling alley, a company co-ed softball game, or even an evening under the stars at a concert. This is a great way to establish relationships which can be extremely beneficial to you over time when you are back in the office.

Shmoozing at the office is a skill that can pay huge dividends. Be very diligent in keeping up with your Shmoozing activities. Do not be a complainer or lazy or disgruntled at work. If you have negative feelings about your work situation, then move on to another job. But while you are at your present position, work hard for your company and on developing your Shmoozing skills.

As we end this chapter, keep in mind that the most important quality you can exude at the office is: energy. How often do you hear people say how tired they are? Be the opposite. You become much more approachable and valuable when you are perceived as energetic. Even if you are very tired, shake it off and act perky, alert and dynamic! You can sleep when you get home. Remember, when you are in the office, do everything you can to appear energetic.

Keep Shmoozing. Be more successful at work. And then Shmooze some more in your personal life!

4

HOW TO SHMOOZE
IN NEGOTIATIONS

We all negotiate every day, whether we know it or not. Some negotiations are formal, like buying a car, and some just occur in the course of a day—like: getting friends to do you a favor picking something up for you at the store or asking your kids to do their chores or getting your spouse to go to the movie you are interested in. Every day, you live through a series of negotiations. Yet, many people never take the time to learn good negotiation techniques. Think about how much more powerful and effective you could be with a strong grasp on how to negotiate effec-tively!

It all comes down to the fact that good negotiation means getting people to see your way of thinking and nothing can help this cause better than the art of the Shmooze.

This chapter will look at some common negotiation situa-tions and how Shmoozing can help you be more successful. This chapter will also look at generic Shmooze techniques that can help in even the simplest negotiations.

The Setup

Before you walk into a negotiation, whether it is a new car purchase, a home purchase or lease, a request for a raise at work, or any number of negotiating situations, you need to prepare yourself and set yourself up with some basics.

First you need to analyze your position and determine exactly what you would like in the best case scenario. If you are buying a car, decide what would be the perfect price for you. If you are buying a house, know exactly what price you would like to pur-chase it for. And, if you are asking for a raise, know precisely how much of a raise you would optimally like.

Next, you also need to determine in advance what you would actually settle for. At what point is the car or house too expen-sive? You have to know your limits up front or you will be nego-tiating in a fog and shooting from the hip. To summarize, you need to know exactly where you stand—what you want and what you will settle for.

Also, determine other bargaining chips that are integral parts of your deal. If you were buying a house, your extra bargaining chips would include who pays closing costs or what extras the seller will consider throwing into the deal, like the washer and dryer or the Jacuzzi. Make a list of all of the bargaining chips and figure out how much they are worth to you. The more chips you can identify, the more room you have to negotiate when the face to face meetings commence. This also gives both parties wriggle room with which to horse trade and come up with a settlement acceptable to both parties. You might disagree on the price, but if they can throw in those few extras you want, you may be happy enough to accept the higher price.

You must do your homework in this area. When buying a house, get comparable sales prices in the area, so you are knowledgeable enough to spot a good deal when you see it. When buying a car, go to a couple of dealers before you sit down and get into serious negotiations. Let them make a couple of offers to you so you know where the price negotiation will really begin. You should get as much information up front as possible so you can feel confident in your decisions and bargaining strategies.

Once you know where you want to guide the negotiations and where you would be happy to see the negotiations end, start to get yourself mentally prepared. Just as suggested everywhere else in this book, your Shmooze techniques need to begin with confidence. You must demonstrate that you really feel like you can get the deal you are requesting. You also must be mentally ready to let the deal go if the other side is too inflexible and the deal is not ending at your predetermined price ranges. Do not get caught up in the object of the negotiations. If the seller is not coming down on price enough for you, just walk away. When you fall psychologically in love with an item you are negotiating for, you lose the bargaining strength that you should have to get a good deal. That is why it is so important to methodically set your limits in advance of the negotiations—both high and low—and force yourself to stick to them. Do not let your emotions move you from your predetermined price goals.

Next, try to identify the goals of your opponent. You know a home seller is trying to get the most for their home, just as the car dealer is trying to get the most for their car. But what secondary motivations can you play on and appeal to in order to help your cause?

In the case of the car dealer, a powerful secondary motivation is the number of cars sold. Dealers are judged by the car manufactures they represent, based on how many units they move. The sales figures are generally tabulated at the end of the month, and often apply to additional rebates they earn from the manufacturers whose cars they sell. For this reason, it is safe to say that a car dealer will let a car go cheaper towards the end of the month because they are often as interested in the sale of one more unit of inventory as much as they are interested in the profit margin from that one car.

With a home seller, their out of pocket expenses may be very important. This knowledge might benefit you if you negotiate to pay closing costs—if they throw in a number of items along with the sale of the house.

A friend of mine offered to pay the closing costs on a house he was buying, which he calculated amounted to about an extra $4,500. In return, he wanted the seller to include his three-year-old Jaguar automobile worth nearly $45,000. The seller countered that he'd throw in the car if the buyer would increase his offer on the house. After the buyer agreed to raise his bid to a higher level than he originally planned, (he purchased the house for about $18,000 more than he thinks he could have gotten it for without the Jaguar in the deal), the deal was done. My friend figures he bought his dream car for $22,500 ($4,500 in closing costs plus $18,000 in additional home cost) even though it was actually worth about $45,000. And, since the car was included in the home purchase, it was absorbed into the mortgage.

So, my friend effectively received a thirty-year loan on a car—since it was part of the mortgage financing. In addition, the mortgage interest one pays is generally tax-deductible! And his mortgage only went up about $80 a month because of the extra $22,500 he paid for the house. Try getting an $80 monthly payment deal on a Jaguar—it is not going to happen to you in this lifetime. But the deal actually gets better. Three years later, my friend sold the house for a nice profit and walked away with the Jaguar. So the $80 payments only lasted him three years! That's what we call creative financing.

The concept here is to determine what motivates the other side. Again, it comes back to identifying the relevant bargaining chips. The more chips you can put into play, the more you can work the deal to your specific liking. So, try to Shmooze your way into getting to know your opponent and their motivations.

The Negotiation Location

When it comes to the actual negotiation, it is time to put your whole Shmooze repertoire to work. Everything from the location, including the mood that you decide to set, to the way you handle the conversation, is integral to you prevailing and getting your way. And getting your way is basically related to all the things we've been teaching you about Shmoozing.

Location

When it comes to location, try to keep the home field advantage. Invite your adversary to come to you so you can control the environment. No matter if the negotiation is in your house, at your place of business, at your attorney's office, or even in a local restaurant, if you are comfortable with the surroundings and if they are foreign to your target, you will have a distinct advantage. You will have much less pressure to hurry, while your adversary will have a subconscious desire to complete the negotiating session and get back to his or her own territory. Typically, the person who is in the bigger hurry will be willing to give in more to end the negotiation. Use this to your advantage and try to schedule the negotiations in surroundings that are familiar and comfortable to you.

This technique is very valuable when trying to get a raise at work. If you just walk into your boss's office and ask for the raise, you will be dealing on enemy ground. Your boss will be comfortable in his/her surroundings and you will have to work that much harder to overcome the lost home court advantage. So use the Shmooze psychology and if you can, schedule an appointment with your boss and request the meeting in a conference room, or even your office or cubical, if it's in a private enough area. If you play your cards right and can manipulate things properly, you will get your boss into your workspace and you will hold the home court advantage. If you hold the meeting in a conference room, at least the territory will be neutral and your likelihood of successful negotiations will be improved.

Your Image in Negotiations

Once you set the meeting location for whatever negotiation you are involved in, the next thing to concentrate on is your image. Analyze your upcoming negotiation and determine what type of image you believe you should exude.

Image

Typically, you will want to look very professional. This will give your adversary the feeling that you are well educated and they will give you more respect and try not to pull anything fast over on you. This respect will probably translate into a more generous first offer than otherwise would happen. But do not overdo it. If you wear your $3,000 Armani suit in to buy a car, it will be tougher for you to get the dealer to cut $200 off of the price of the car. They will assume you are obviously wealthy and have the dough and therefore, they may decide to dig in their heals, trying even harder to get more money out of you. This is all because of the image message you've projected.

Every situation is different, so spend some time analyzing your upcoming negotiation and consider what kind of image would help you the most. Then, do everything you can do to display that strategic image. It will pay huge dividends in the final results.

Break the Ice

You finally meet your adversary face to face. What is the very first thing you should do?

You should apply all your Shmooze techniques to the circumstances at hand. These negotiations are no different than all of the other situations discussed in this book. You are trying to talk someone into giving you something at a lower price than they would like it to be actually worth. You are trying to create a working relationship with your adversary which will result in you getting the best deal you can get. You are going to Shmooze this target and psyche them out using everything we're teaching you.

Now it is time for you to use all of your Shmooze skills.

Ice Breaking

Smile and introduce yourself to your target. Then, begin with some small talk. As discussed in Chapter 2 – "Shmooze Basics" you want to initially create a conversation that is off the topic. You are there to negotiate, but first go off that topic and discuss some other non-threatening subject that will spark some interest in your target. If they love golf, and you can get a golf conversation going, you are well on your way. Once the target starts to like you, and is a little impressed by something about you, they will be more trusting and more willing to give in to some of your requests and to tell you a straighter story about whatever it is that they are selling. So, start off with some small talk and try to keep the topic on something your target is truly interested in.

Throughout this process, do not lose sight of some of the other Shmooze techniques discussed previously. You should work in everything from eye contact to humor and charm—all of these methods can be extremely valuable.

Ice Breaking Tips

- *Small talk*
- *Eye contact*
- *Humor*
- *Charm*
- *Shmooze Basics from Chapter 2*

Your goals in negotiations are very similar to your goals when meeting someone at a party. You want to bond with them and create a new relationship quickly. If you can convert them into someone who likes you and can sense your warmth and charisma, the negotiations will be that much more amenable and successful.

Get Down to Business

Once you feel you have made a connection with your negotiating partner, it is time to get down to business. Make a transition from the small talk to the negotiation gently, with a line similar to, "We think we really want to discuss actually buying your house—I'm anxious to see what kind of deal we can make." Any line that shows you are interested and upbeat will be an effective psychological shift here. Once everyone has changed gears and is ready to get down to business, keep on Shmoozing. Never let yourself get distracted by the process. You want to beam friendliness, confidence and charisma at every turn, no matter which way the negotiations head.

When actually involved in the negotiation process the two key things to keep in mind is to keep your speaking style simple and specific. You do not need to impress your adversary with your knowledge of big words or technical terms. There is no need to call the maid's room the "chambermaid's quarters", or the garbage man a "waste disposal engineer", and there is no reason to throw out fancy terms or concepts that are over your target's head. If you use fancy logic, they will probably need to ask you for clarification or stay silent and then be wary of future topics you will be discussing in negotiations. You will create an unnecessarily awkward atmosphere by choosing to use intellectual sounding words or fancy, high concepts. Your target will feel less intelligent and whenever that happens they will be suspicious about whether they are equipped to play on your level. Do you really have to start discussing the trend in the 30-year-bond-interest rate fluctuation, or the change in the yield curve? Do you want them to call their lawyer or accountant to do the negotiating with you? We didn't think so! So keep it simple.

You want to keep your target always feeling confident and comfortable that they can handle themselves negotiating with you. If you put on too much of a show with your intellectualism, and sophisticated knowledge about what you are negotiating over, they might feel inferior and become afraid to carry out further negotiations. Remember, it is your job as the savvy Shmoozer to keep everyone who is involved feeling comfortable about the conversation and the negotiations. You should consider it your responsibility to be the good host—the master Shmoozer—and keep everyone happy.

In addition to keeping your linguistics simple, you also want to keep your words specific. Say what you mean. If you couch your requests in hypothetical situations or generalities, your meaning can be lost. For instance, do not tell a home seller you are interested in "some of the living room furniture." Be specific about which pieces you are interested in and how you propose these pieces should financially affect the deal.

Also, as we discussed in Chapter 2– "Basic Shmoozing", use buzzwords that are tailored to your adversary. If you can sound like you're comfortable living in their world, you will immediately gain their admiration and trust. Additionally, If you're up against an intelligent negotiating target, you should feel free to use your opponent's buzzwords. This will instantly make them aware that you are educated and will serve to tip them that they should not even think about trying try to take advantage of you. They will also most likely make you a more generous first offer than they otherwise would, since they realize they will not be able to easily take advantage of you.

Another technique you should employ in your initial negotiations and conversations is to be a good listener. You can control the negotiations without having to talk the entire time. You will learn more about your target's needs, wants, and goals by listening to them. Let them talk. You will always get your chance.

To Get Down To Business You Must:
- *Make a connection*
- *Keep it simple*
- *Be sure your target is comfortable*
- *Be specific*
- *Use your target's buzzwords*
- *Be a good listener*

Getting the Facts
During negotiations there is a lot of information gathering you can do. For example, if you are buying a car, you might want the dealer to tell you about maintenance histories, or resale value.

If you are negotiating to buy a house, you might want to know about schools, kids in the neighborhood, or crime statistics. To glean this information you can use two types of questions: "Open-ended" questions and "Specific questions".

Early in the negotiations, you can use open-ended questions to learn about general items. For example, you can ask if crime is an issue in the neighborhood. The specific version of this question would be, "Can you tell me about any recent instances when the police were called to the neighborhood?" The more specific the questions, the more concrete information you can learn.

On the other hand, though, general questions can open up information topics that you might not have thought of. For example, if during a home purchase negotiation you ask the home seller if the home has required any maintenance expenses recently, the seller might ramble a bit and give you a list of problems they had fixed such as, a leaky roof, termites or hidden cracks in the foundation. If you had asked specifically if the home has a leaky roof, you might get the honest answer, but you would have missed the more important information about the termites and the cracked foundation.

Use both general and specific questions strategically throughout the negotiation process and you will uncover all the information you need in order to bargain from an informed position of strength. Lastly, it is important that you are never condescending when asking questions. Try to put a positive slant on everything and do not be antagonistic or judgmental when asking your questions. You are more likely to get the truth this way, and you'll often learn more than the target ever intended to tell you.

How to Ask For What You Want

Before you ask for exactly what you want, work on expectation building. Let us say you take your car to an auto mechanic and he gives you an initial estimate of $400. Then, when you go to pick up your car, he charges you only $300. You feel great. You were prepared to spend the $400 and the perception is that you just "saved" $100, instead of you having just spent $300.

You can use this same trick in your negotiations. While you lay out your position, give the other party the impression they are in for an offer that is not up to their expectation. But, when you finally give them your best offer, it should be better than the low ball bid that they were expecting from you. You can be sure it will be met with a much more positive feeling from your adversary than the very low offer you had initially led them to believe you intended to make. They will probably try and work you up even further, but at least they are feeling better about your offer and this good feeling will work to your advantage, when you finally do settle on a price.

Set the expectations of your opponent, and then build your case with as many facts and figures as you can. Slowly explain your position and why your upcoming offer is fair, well thought out, and justified.

Deadlines

When you finish a negotiating session, you will probably leave with some homework items that you are supposed to move on. You are supposed to think about the offer and call them back the next day; or you had promised to put together the paperwork showing the permits for the house addition; or you will try and arrange outside financing for the car; etc.

Just remember to live up to any promises you make. Even if you decide to cancel the deal, call and tell your adversary that. You can do absolutely no good by blowing off deadlines, or missing them, while you try and put promised materials together. If you find a deadline impossible to meet, call and explain what the problem is and profusely apologize. Your opponent will be able to sense if you are being truthful or just stalling. Your courtesy and honesty will pay dividends down the road.

Personality Quirks

During your negotiations, stay relaxed and confident. Use all of your Shmooze skills to maintain eye contact, listen intently, bond with your adversary, and work your way into the power position. While you are in the heart of the negotiations, avoid personality quirks like being fidgety, interrupting your adversary, using bad public speaking crutches like saying "um" or having long awkward pauses.

Additionally, avoid getting angry at all costs. If your adversary is obnoxious and is raising your blood pressure—work around this distraction by trying to be logical and calmly explaining your position and situation. If you are getting nowhere, simply make your offer and see if you can then start a concrete discussion from there.

If you become agitated and end up angry with your negotiating partner, the only result will be that both parties become incapable of coming to a successful conclusion of the negotiations. Alternatively, you can politely thank your adversary and move on. If you leave on good terms, you can keep the door open for later negotiations when your adversary is in a better mood or realizes your offer was the best that they've gotten so far. This is the strategically intelligent way to proceed.

Counter-Offers

A friend of mine pointed out a counter-offer technique that just begs to make the negotiating situation awkward and uncomfortable. But that is the goal of the technique and it is actually very successful. Here's how it goes: Let's say you have offered to sell your car for $4,000 and your buyer has countered at $3,000. My friend's philosophy is that whoever speaks next will lose out on the opportunity of getting the best possible deal from his adversary.

The next thing said will typically be a counter to the counter-offer and one of the parties will be giving in. The point is to not be the party who is giving in. You can end up with an awkward silence that can fully last minutes. Wait your opponent out and you'll do better in the long run.

I have been with my friend on his sales calls (he sells high end cigars) and I have seen this technique in action. The tension during the silence is intense and very uncomfortable, even for me as an observer. But, the cigar buyer usually ends up speaking first and giving up something either on price or quantity.

A less dramatic ploy is to know your limits and anticipate the counter-offer. You will then be ready to make a case for your side and then re-counter with some offer that is within your guidelines. This method will be more endearing and help you with future calls on the same adversary. You let them know that this is the most you can offer and that you'll, regrettably, have to pass if more money is required. Period. Now it is up to them to save the negotiations with a compromise, or to end the discussions because of their intransigence or inflexibility.

First Moves

You have probably already been in this situation: You meet up with someone selling something and you ask, "How much?" The person replies, "I'm not sure. What do you think it is worth?" You want to avoid the "not sure" problem at any cost. If you are selling, know what you will ask for your item and then do not be shy—or embarrassed—to ask it.

If you are buying and confronted with this problem, quickly tell them what you think it is worth. You need to get the conversation going. You do not want to be stuck in an "I don't know, what do you think it's worth?" battle.

Last Moves

The negotiation is over and you have come to an understanding that you are both happy with. Now what do you do?

The key is to cement the deal and leave with no ambiguities. The best way to accomplish this is to thank your opponent, express your excitement and satisfaction, and then summarize all the points you agreed on. Take the extra five minutes to officially reiterate the agreement. This will make everyone more comfortable that there are no misunderstandings and will help cement the entire agreement. You can never be too clear at the end of a negotiating meeting. You want to ensure that when you reconvene to sign off on the contracts or whatever the next step is in your deal, you do not end up with a problem that could have been avoided through a simple summarization.

Summary

You are now armed with all the tools you'll need to be an effective negotiator. Combine your Shmoozing skills with these business skills and you are sure to improve your chances for getting a great deal.

5

HOW TO IMPRESS THEM

Charisma

You are sitting around with a group of friends talking about the party you went to the night before. Someone says, "That guy Dave was so funny!" Then everyone agrees and begins talking about how impressed they were by Dave. The question is, What did Dave do to get everyone talking the next day? If you asked around about this phenomenon the answer you will usually receive is something like, "That guy just has this great energy around him. When he walks in a room everyone notices." People usually cannot put their finger on a reason why someone stands out during a social or business situation. The most common tangible reasons are humor, intelligence, and appearance, but these are neither guarantees nor are they the key components to success.

No matter what situation you are in, business or social, the key to being the person everyone remembers the next day is in the art of the Shmooze. Use your newly developed confidence and some of the basic Shmoozing techniques to impress those around you, and people will remember you. Begin by using all of the major tools discussed in the last chapter: from Confidence to Eye contact to Humor.

These basic Shmoozing techniques used together build your personality into one that exudes charisma. The Shmoozing creates those positive moments and when people get a lot of positive moments from talking with you, a positive image begins to burn into their psyche which translates into your appearing charismatic. Your humor, interest in their conversations, and penetrating eyes create charisma. With the charisma flowing, you are well on your way to being remembered and talked about the next day.

The next step is to also impress them.

Leave an Impression

You are at a party, using your basic Shmooze techniques smoothly and masterfully and you are feeling good. Now you can add some extra MAI's (Make An Impression) to clinch the deal and make yourself unforgettable. These positive impression enhancers are in the form of tricks that will thoroughly impress people. They will only take you about five minutes each to master, making this the smartest five minutes you will ever spend!

Practice these tricks a couple of times and they will look so amazing that people will ask you to repeat them over and over. A quick word of advice would be not to repeat the tricks for the same audience. The more you repeat them, the more likely someone will figure out what you are doing and then the whole illusion and positive impression will be minimized.

Pool Tricks

If there is a pool table at your social engagement (bar, someone's house, etc.) you are five minutes away from the entire party wanting to talk to you. What follows are ten pool shots that require absolutely no pool skill at all. Merely learn where to place the pool balls and you are in for an instant great impression and lots of attention at any party.

The Borlaug '81 Corvette Special

Legend has it this shot was named after a hustler who won a Corvette by sinking this shot in a Cincinnati pool hall, even though the shot could not be any easier. Imagine placing six balls on the pool table, then setting down the cue ball. You take one masterful shot, and all six balls fly off into different pockets. You have skillfully cleared the table of all the balls while the white ball slows to a stop. Everyone watching will be thoroughly amazed at your talents. You create another positive moment, and this time it is huge. You will want to be ready with one or two more trick shots because it is inevitable that your new fans and friends will beg you for more.

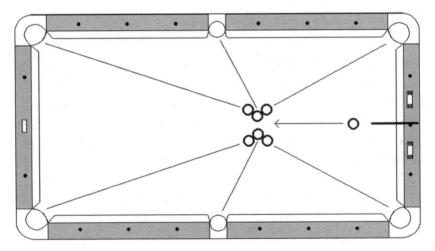

The Borlaug '81 Corvette Special

How It's Done:

The Borlaug Special requires that you merely place the six balls correctly. No pool skill is required. Follow the diagram below for the ball placement and then shoot the cue ball directly down the middle with a nice, firm shot. Presto! Like magic! Six balls—all sunk—all in different pockets. People will start calling you Minnesota Fats. Members of the opposite sex will begin fawning over you. Business associates will be shocked. Bosses will be impressed.

This shot helped Steve and I Shmooze one of the most controversial people alive today. We were both asked to attend a party at O.J. Simpson's house to tape a segment for our new television show. This party was after his acquittal and created quite a stir, with picketers outside his Rockingham estate and television helicopters circling overhead. O.J. was polite but very reserved during the evening because he knew he was the subject of more attention than ever. We knew that we had to do something special to get the television footage we needed for our show.

Bret and Steve with O.J. Simpson (At O.J.'s Rockingham Estate).

While near O.J.'s pool table, I announced to all who were close by, including the "Juice" himself, that I could sink six balls, all into different pockets, with one shot. My ploy worked and O.J. replied, with the whole room looking at us, "I'd like to see that."

I set up the Borlaug Special and—BAM—the balls all slammed into their proper pockets, making me one very popular man in a party full of total strangers (that I had crashed with a little help from our TV show's producers!)

O.J. was thoroughly impressed and asked me to teach him the shot. The Shmooze worked wonderfully and we got our television footage.

The Nuclear Grand Swagelgale Shot

Who knows where the name of this shot came from, but it is very effective nevertheless. You need to practice this shot a dozen times before you try it as a Shmooze technique in a real situation. You will be surprised at how fast you can pick it up. This trick looks so impressive because the cue ball actually changes direction and comes back on its own to knock in the eight ball. The following diagram shows how to set this trick up. Hit the cue ball straight down and towards the far corner pocket. The cue ball will knock in the ball leaning against the near pocket,

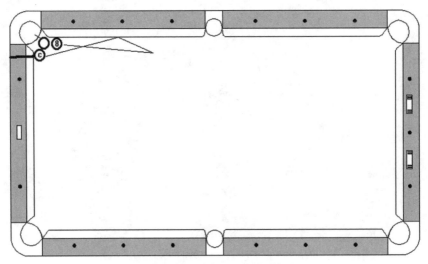

Nuclear Grand Swagelgale Shot

then it will hit the bumper, and finally spin backwards (because you hit down on the ball), and then it will hit the eight ball in. This is an awesome trick.

My partner Steve and I attended a celebrity pool tournament at the Hollywood Athletic Club at Universal Studios. Steve made this interesting shot and was an instant star among the attendees. People who complimented him included actors Steve Baldwin and Rob Lowe.

Three months later we were at a New Year's Eve party in New York. Jeff Goldblum, who we had not even noticed was at the party, approached us and said he had seen the incredible pool shot Steve had made in Los Angeles at the celebrity tournament. He asked if we could give him some pool lessons sometime in L.A. I told him that we were the wrong people to ask for lessons, but if he wanted us to show him some trick shots, we would be happy to do so while we were all in New York. Steve and I met up with Jeff and two of his friends the next day at a local pool hall in New York City and we taught him five or six of our best trick shots.

The point is that everyone loves trick pool shots. People just cannot stop being amazed when they see so many balls fly perfectly into the pockets. If you learn these shots, you have a serious weapon in your arsenal during Shmoozing opportunities. Use them to your advantage and you will be remembered the next day by whoever was in the room—guaranteed.

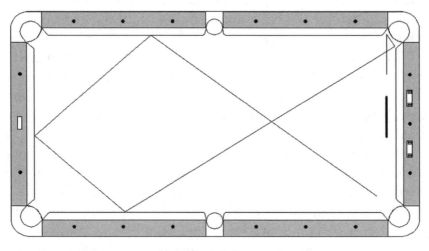

Mega Bank-A-Rooney

Mega Bank-A-Rooney

People love to see bank shots. This is a five banker that knocks in the eight ball. Once again merely line up the balls in the right spot as indicated in the diagram above, and you will have no trouble sinking the shot. You look good, people are impressed, and the successful Shmooze continues.

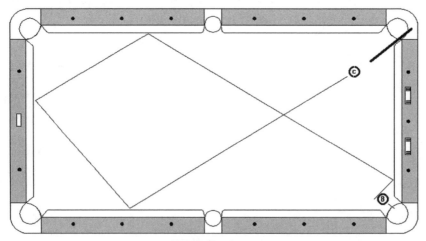

Bolero Banker

Bolero Banker

Here again is a bank shot. It banks four times, but when it sinks the eight ball, the "kiss" is impressive. Look at the diagram on the left. When the cue ball kisses off of the eight ball it drops it into the pocket. This is a great shot for romantics.

Bret with Jeff Goldblum (At a movie premier).

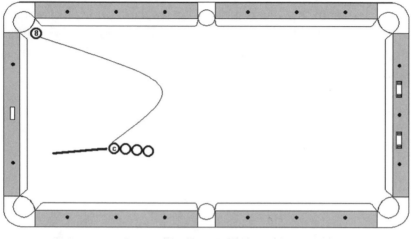

Left Turn Clyde

Left Turn Clyde

This shot really looks unbelievable. It is tough to get the pool stick out of the way in time, but with a little practice you will get the hang of it. This one is impressive because people love to see a curve. When you hit the cue ball the three other balls will shoot towards the far right corner pocket, The cue will curve around and hit the eight ball. Practice up and then do what you do best and Shmooze away.

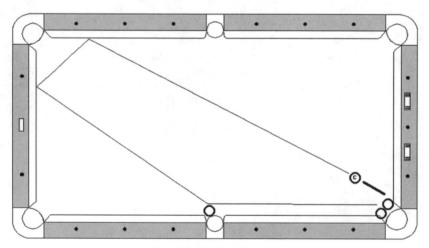

Athenian Number Three

Steve with Sylvester Stallone (At a Fundraiser sponsored by Marvin Davis).

The Athenian Number Three

Again, you need to really practice this shot. It even helps to practice on the table you are going to attempt it on. As with all of the other shots, this one doesn't take any skill, just a little trial and error on the table to see just where to shoot the ball. The diagram to the left and below will get you very close the first time.

I made this unusual shot in front of Sylvester Stallone at the Planet Hollywood in Beverly Hills. It is amazing how impressed people get because you can hit a trick shot. They automatically assume you are a great pool player and start treating you like an Olympic champion, when in fact, knowing where to line up the balls and how to aim your shot is really the only skill needed. Sylvester Stallone absolutely loved this trick shot and asked me to show him a few more. I have met up with Stallone a dozen

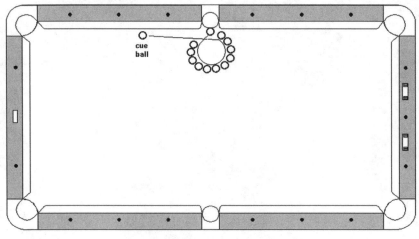

Lee Edward Norman Ring Shot

times since at various events and parties and he always introduces me to his friends at whatever function we're at as "Mr. Pool."

Lee Edward Norman Ring Shot

It's time to make their eyes pop out of their heads. This shot is very easy to do, yet incredibly impressive. Make sure you practice a little bit beforehand. You want to hit the second ball in the circle, just barely. Hit it as softly as possible, but with enough force to get around the circle. Also make sure each of the balls

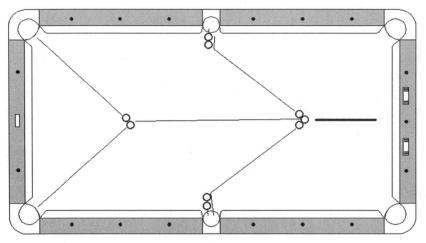

Capital Grill Trick Shot

in the circle are against each other, as indicated in the above-left diagram.

Capital Grill Trick Shot

A regular at the Capital Grill in Miami taught me this trick shot, which sinks eight balls in one shot. I love this trick because after practicing it several times, I had it down and can duplicate it perfectly at any social event. Any time you can sink eight balls on a pool table in one shot, everyone who sees it will be impressed. And impressed = Positive Moment = Successful Shmooze.

I strongly suggest that you learn all of these pool tricks so you have the use of these additional powerful weapons in your personal Shmoozing arsenal. Practice them and then go to work Shmoozing with even greater success!

Magic Tricks

Unfortunately, there will not always be a pool table around when you are trying to Shmooze. Luckily, there is another genre of MAIs (Make An Impression) that works just as well—it's called Magic. If you have any doubt about it, just ask David Copperfield, who managed to Shmooze his way into the heart of Claudia Schiffer through his magic. While speaking to David at a recent party, he told us that magic has a way of breaking the ice that no other Shmoozing method affords. It really is a fact that people just love magic. They enjoy suspending belief while watching incredible, impossible feats of magic being performed. Even those who say they do not like magic, will end up being impressed if shown a good trick.

For those of us Shmoozers who do not want to spend the next three years perfecting our sleight of hand techniques, the following tricks are simple enough to do immediately and create that instant positive moment that is so important to your successful Shmooze. So, study these tricks and prepare to Shmooze away. With even greater success!

The "Stripper Deck" of Cards

Some of the easiest tricks to do can be performed with a "stripper deck" of cards, which can be purchased at any magic shop for about ten dollars. With the stripper deck, you can do hundreds of tricks, but you only need to master three or four and you will become a legend at parties and events. The next three tricks are done easily with the stripper deck.

The Old "Find The Card" Trick

The easiest trick to perform with the stripper deck is the classic "Find The Card" trick. Shuffle the special deck thoroughly. Fan the deck face down and then ask an audience member to pick a card. Tell them not to show you the card, and next tell

Bret with David Copperfield (At the Golden Globe Awards).

them to replace the card anywhere in the deck. You will then be able to immediately slide that very same card out of the deck and state, "Is this your card?" impressing the heck out of observers with your amazing skills, time and again.

How It's Done:

The trick is in the stripper deck. The deck is slightly tapered, one end of the deck is slightly smaller in width than the other end. It is unnoticeable to anyone handling the cards, but it allows you to group cards together, or keep track of the location of a card. When all of the slightly tapered cards are setup one way, and one card is reversed in the deck, the reversed card is easy to find because the wide end of the card that was just inserted back into the deck by your audience member, is slightly protruding at the narrow end of the deck. Because of this, you can then easily spot and pull out of the deck the reversed card.

During this trick, while the audience member is holding and looking at the card they just selected, you discreetly reverse the direction of the deck. When they replace the card back into the deck, the slightly wider end of the selected card is locatable at the narrow end of the deck, allowing you to easily find the card without anyone knowing how you masterfully did it.

The Flying Funai

Here's what the audience sees: You shuffle the deck completely. You show the cards face up and all of the cards are mixed up—reds, blacks, numbers, face cards, everything. The deck is thoroughly shuffled. You flip the cards back over so they are face down and cut the deck three times. You then flip the deck back over and you have magically separated all the cards. All of the black cards are together and all of the red cards are together. I saw some magician do this trick on *The Tonight Show with Johnny Carson* and Johnny almost popped out of his seat in amazement.

How It's Done:

In the Flying Funai trick, you are still using the special deck that is slightly tapered. So, before you perform the trick you simply have to reverse the position of all the red cards in the deck, placing them all so that their wide ends are reversed and thereby slightly protruding out of the thin side of the deck. Because of this positioning, when you cut the deck you can easily pull all the wider red cards out and put them on the top of the deck. When you flip the deck over you will therefore find all the reds in one section and all the blacks in another. As long as you reverse each red card so the wider part of the card is in the area where all of the thin cards are, you will be able to perform this trick flawlessly.

The Super Flying Funai

For an added twist to the Flying Funai, show the audience that the cards are all mixed up. Flip them back over so they are face down. Fan the deck and ask someone to pick a card. Let us say they picked the four of hearts (red). You do not let them show you the card, but after they have picked their card and looked at it, you should cut the deck a few times to separate the reds and blacks just as you did in the previous trick. Then reverse the deck and have them replace the card, anywhere they want in the deck. Then cut the deck a few more times. Then, as you show the cards to the audience, all of the red cards are together and all of the black cards are together. The one exception is the card they chose, the four of hearts, which is standing out like a sore thumb in the middle of the black cards. Wow! A serious audience pleaser. You have successfully Shmoozed the entire room by the time this trick is done.

At a party in Hollywood, I was showing the Super Flying Funai trick to a number of people, including actor Andy Garcia. Andy came up to me afterwards and asked me if I could teach him the trick. Naturally, being the Shmoozer I am, I taught it to him and he was amazed at how simple it was. He offered to buy my stripper deck from me, but I took advantage of a good Shmoozing opportunity and graciously gave him the deck. I watched him performing the trick for friends later that evening and was his special buddy for the rest of the party. That simple deck of cards got me introduced to all of Andy's friends at the party and allowed me to exchange phone numbers with this celebrity whom I had admired for years.

Because of this successful Shmooze, I became an equal with someone I had always wanted to hang out with. (Come to think of it, I'll bet I was the star, as far as Andy was concerned, and he probably felt he was lucky to be hanging out with me!)

Remember, however, that when it comes to magic tricks with small groups of people, everyone will always ask how you did it. Do not give in to temptation and tell them. Once they know the secret of the tapered deck, you lose the positive moment you had. The crowd is not impressed anymore once they see how easy it is to perform a particular trick. Sometimes it's fun to be the teacher, sometimes it's even a useful Shmooze to teach them how it's done. But when dealing with magic I find it is usually best not to succumb to temptation and to keep the secrets to yourself. In the case of Andy Garcia, I balanced the lost magic trick moment with the Shmooze opportunity to bond with him. The opportunity to please Andy seemed to be more valuable to

Bret with Andy Garcia (At fundraiser sponsored by Marvin Davis).

me than the magic trick's positive moment. This turned out to be a wise move on my part because Andy and I hung out together for the balance of the party. For the most part, though, it is better to leave them impressed with the trick, wondering how you did it. Lastly, never explain your trick to the whole crowd. No good can ever come of that. You effectively give up the illusion and lose the positive moment, and you receive no bonding benefits back because you will not be able to bond with the entire audience. And once they learn how easy it can be to perform certain tricks, you lose your special status and become a mere common mortal again.

When you buy a stripper deck at the magic store, it will come with complete instructions and usually about a hundred additional tricks that you can perform. Pick out several others and practice them and you will be on your way to Shmoozing with the best of us.

Bite the Quarter Trick

You give your target a quarter and ask him or her to warm it up with their breath. Tell him or her that you will bite the quarter in half, but they need to warm it up so it is softer. After your target breaths on the quarter and hands it back to you, test it by squeezing it and act disappointed. Tell him or her to forget the whole thing since they obviously are not prepared to put the proper effort into the trick. He or she will say, "Ok, Ok, let me try again." You hold out the quarter and let them blow on it. You then bite the quarter in half, showing them the incredible remaining half. Then you blow on the quarter and instantly it reverts back to a whole quarter.

This trick is simply done with another magic shop prop. You can purchase the bending quarter for about fifteen dollars.

How It's Done:

The way the trick actually works is as follows: you hand the target an actual quarter. No matter how well they blow, nothing will happen. When you get disgusted and retrieve the quarter from the targeted person, you put it in your pocket. Then you ask them if they are able to blow harder? When the target offers to try harder, you then pull out the special bending quarter. You hold the bending quarter and let them blow a couple more times. Then you can bite the special quarter, actually bending the top half down behind the bottom half. Hold the quarter up to the amazement of your target. Then blow at the quarter and at the same time release the bent top half. It will spring back in shape and the viewer will be astonished. It is just amazing how effective a simple fifteen dollar trick can be to your Shmoozing activities. Suddenly, you are the darling of the room and you have endeared yourself to all who have witnessed your great talent. Trust us, this stuff all works. We do it over and over again and look where it got us! Shmooze on!

The Pen Through the Dollar Trick

You show your audience a pen and a dollar bill. Better yet, ask anyone in the audience to loan you a dollar, so they are sure you are not using a trick dollar bill. Once you have the dollar, explain that you are going to drive the pen through the face of George Washington. Once everyone is ready, and you have inspired the proper amount of anticipation, you slam the pen down through the face of George Washington on the dollar. You hold up the pen showing the skewered bill on the pen. You then tell the audience that you will fix the bill. Tell them to watch the pen carefully. One of your hands holds the skewered dollar, and the other holds the pen which is skewering the dollar. You yank the pen out of the dollar, and, Presto, the dollar is intact, with no hole. You can let the audience inspect the dollar and the pen and they will find nothing fishy. It's amazing!

How It's Done:

After a quick trip to your local magic shop, and another fifteen dollar purchase, you can do this trick five minutes after opening the box—no skill required. The key is in the pen—which is actually a trick pen in two pieces. Just above the writing tip of the pen, the shaft of the pen comes apart. When apart, the pen looks like it has been broken into two pieces—a small piece which includes the writing tip and about a half an inch of the shaft, and a larger piece which includes the rest of the shaft to the clicker. A very strong magnet holds the two pieces of the pen together, making it look like a real pen.

To perform the trick you show the connected pen to the audience. It looks completely real. You then place the dollar bill laying flat on your left hand, over your parted fingers. You explain that you are going to slam the pen down into the dollar and drive a hole through George Washington with a tomahawk-like stabbing motion (starting with the pen held up high near your head and then proceeding down into the bill in your hand). Then, while continuing to talk, after you've demonstrated the stabbing motion in the air, you start the trick by placing the pen laying down in your left hand. Place the dollar bill in its position over your parted fingers holding it in place with your thumb on top. At this point, the bill should also be covering and on top of half of the pen that's lying flat in your open palm and on your fingers. As you lift the pen up with your right hand, use your thumb to hold the bottom section of the pen firmly by pressing on the dollar that's on top of it. Your grip will allow the magnets to release the pen halves.

Now lift the top half of the pen up to your head as if you were holding a knife, and stab down at George's head. Once the pen hits the bill the magnets will again connect with half the pen, re-attaching itself under the dollar and half above the dollar. The illusion of a skewered bill will be complete. Lift the pen up and show everyone that the pen is now completely through the dollar. They will not be impressed yet because they figure all you did was drive a pen through the dollar! Now comes the amazing part. Hold a corner of the bill with your left hand and hold the end of the pen with your right hand. Have the writing end of the pen pointing directly towards the audience so they can see the pen tip and the full dollar bill. Yank the pen straight back and the magnets let the dollar escape but keep the pen connected. While the audience is inspecting the dollar, in disbelief that there is no hole, put the pen in your pocket. If someone asks to see the pen, pull out the identical normal pen that comes with the trick. No skill required, just a terrific prop from the magic shop and some smooth, savvy Shmoozing on your part.

These three props are inexpensive and allow you to perform utterly amazing tricks that will impress and astonish almost any group. The Shmooze potential is huge. After doing some of these tricks, we guarantee you that people will be talking about you the next day. Make the minor investment. Try the tricks by yourself once or twice and you will be ready to suddenly be the life of your next social gathering, attracting more attention than you know what to do with.

Magic Paper Clips

You show your audience two paper clips, a rubber band and a dollar bill. You place the rubber band around the bill, then fold the bill. You place a paper clip on the fold to hold it in place. Then fold the bill a second time, and paper clip the fold. Then, as the audience watches, you grab the two corners of the bill and snap it open. The paper clips have magically linked themselves together and are dangling from the rubber band.

How It's Done:

You loop a rubber band around the thinner side of a dollar bill. It should be of a size slightly larger than the bill so that part of the band hangs below the bill. You fold 1/3 of the length of the bill from the left side of the bill, over towards the right and middle of the bill. Place one of the paper clips over this fold at the top of the bill. Make sure the paper clip is snug against the edge (the end) of the bill and placed near the edge of the folded piece and over the number that shows the bill's value (near the middle of the bill).

Then turn the bill completely around so you are looking at the back of the bill (not upside down). The paper clip should still be at the top. Now fold the other edge of the bill towards the center.

Put the other paper clip (from the top of the bill) over the piece you just folded and the middle of the bill, clipping them together, as you had done previously to the other third of the bill; at the edge over the bill's number that shows it's value. (Do not put the clip over the first folded section.) The band should be hanging down from the middle of the bill at this point. Then grip the bill at its top edges (near the numbers) and yank the bill open. The rubber band will still be around the middle of the bill, but the paper clips, connected to each other, will be dangling from the rubber band.

If you practice this you'll better understand how and why it works. It sounds complicated but it is actually quite simple to perform.

Psychic Change

Take out all the change in your pocket (preferably between 8 and 16 coins). Toss all the change on the table. Turn your back and tell someone to turn over a coin. Then tell them to turn over another coin. Then another one. Then a pair of coins. Then tell them to turn over any two coins they want. They can continue to turn over pairs of coins for as long as they like. When they are through, tell them to cover one of the coins with their hand. You turn around and tell them whether the covered coin is heads or tails.

The trick is to count the heads showing when you first throw down your change. Make sure there is an even number of heads. If there is not, turn one tail over to create an even number of heads. Once there is an even number of heads, you can progress with the trick. When you turn around after your volunteer flips the coins, count the heads. If there is an even number of heads, the covered coin is tails. If there is an odd number of heads, the covered coin is heads. It is magic! And trust us, as usual, the reaction of your targeted person to your masterfullness will be amazement and respect.

Cooking and Shmoozing

When you are trying to Shmooze a particular person, cooking for them is an almost unbeatable idea. If you can cook up a nice meal, the positive moments will come fast and furiously!

While it is nice to take someone out to a special dinner at a fancy restaurant, cooking for them yourself shows effort, caring, and the importance to you of the person you invited to the dinner. The old saying that a Hallmark card is nice, but can never beat a homemade card, is so true. And the analogy holds perfectly when you choose to cook for someone. Whether the dinner is for business, pleasure or romance, you can create a serious Shmooze opportunity by taking the trouble to do dinner the homemade way. Not only will you have your intended target as a captive audience, you will also build up a reservoir of good will that you will be able to tap in the future.

This is a win-win situation, no matter how you look at it, unless you screw up the meal. Do not get too creative. Cook something you have made before so there is no risk of a kitchen disaster!

The Atmosphere In Your Home

The big three to be concerned about when it comes to atmosphere are: cleanliness, flowers, and the enchanting smell of fresh baked cookies.

First and foremost, make sure your home is clean. It can never be too clean. Clean, Clean, Clean. And if my point is not clear enough, you might want to spend some time and concentrate on cleaning. Either hire a cleaning person for the day, or break out the rubber gloves and do it yourself, but make sure your place is spotless. Your guest will surely notice any areas that you forgot to clean or decided to cut corners and did not clean, so just do not miss any parts. Be very thorough. OK, I'm done being your mom.

Let us now examine the second of the big three in atmosphere: flowers. No matter who you are or who you are trying to impress, you can usually create a positive moment through utilizing the power of fresh flowers. Guys, you should not feel too weird about flowers as a florist can help you with nice masculine arrangements that will compliment the color scheme in your home and help set the mood—whether business or romantic. A couple of well placed and well planned arrangements can really add to the decor of every home. Additionally, the fact that you have flowers in your home gives the guest the impression that you put time and effort into setting up the dinner. You become the well prepared host in the eyes of your guest. (Needless to say, if someone else gave you the flowers as a gift, be sure that the card is not attached to the flowers or lying around anywhere near them. This can undo the mood you've created and "bust your rap" immediately!)

So, you have cleaned your place and set out some fresh flowers. Now it is time for the big atmospheric *Coup de Gras*: the smell of fresh baked cookies. Ten minutes before your guests are due to arrive, drop a chunky hunk of cookie dough into a prewarmed oven. The smell of baking cookies will fill your home with a special folksy feeling of home cooking and warmth. Shazam! You are in like Flynn. Your house looks good and smells good and consequently, you are looking better than ever in the eyes of your targeted person.

The Dinner

The atmosphere is set and it is time to concentrate on the dinner. If you are a good cook, you have no problem. Make your specialty. When you are trying to impress someone, it is never a good time to experiment. Fall back on a tried and true recipe and make sure you prepare it well. If you are not too swift in the kitchen, like Steve and I, and your only expertise in cooking is warming up Brown Sugar Cinnamon Pop-Tarts, then the next few paragraphs are for you.

The key to creating an impressive meal that helps with your Shmooze can be found in two words: Seafood Pasta. For a main course try the following recipe for a seafood pasta. It is almost impossible to screw up and is an impressive dish that appears complicated to prepare, creating the desired impression that you have been slaving away for that special person.

You cannot stop at the main course. You need to move on to equally impressive side dishes. But for the rest of the dinner,

SEAFOOD PASTA

10 Strips of Bacon
½ Pound Raw Shrimp (Shelled & Deveined)
½ Pound Scallops
½ Pound Crab Meat
1 Red Onion Chopped
1 Package Pasta

Fry bacon until done. Remove from pan. Add shrimp, scallops, crab & onion to bacon drippings in pan. Fry 10 minutes, stirring often. Season with garlic, salt, lemon and pepper.

Cook pasta according to its package instructions. Toss with seafood mixture. (Modify ingredients to your taste. If you don't like bacon, use cooking oil. If you can't find one seafood ingredient, double up on one of the other ones).

This dish Serves 8 to 10 people. Cut ingredients in half for 4 to 5 people.

there is no law that says you have to cook it all yourself. Stop by your local full service grocery store if you don't have time to do the deed yourself, and pick up a loaf of fresh garlic bread and side dishes from the deli. You can complete the meal with store bought items and still honestly claim you are the great chef who prepared this awesome meal. After all, you did create the main course and that is what people will really focus on when they begin evaluating your meal. (Be sure to throw out all of the containers and bags from the deli. Dump them out of your house so they are not accidently seen by your date, if she or he happens to help you clean up! This "evidence" could destroy your carefully honed image and make you look like a fraud!)

Alcohol

While you are carefully planning out the dinner experience, do not forget the spirits. Whether you serve wine, hard liquor,

or both, you need to be prepared. An overview is included below. In addition, we have prepared a number of the recipes for
the more popular drinks in Appendix A at the back of this book.
A savvy host or hostess should be able to serve their guests most
of these drinks without too much of a struggle. If worst comes
to worst and you are not sure how to make the drink someone
is asking for, just discreetly refer to this book for the recipe, and
everyone will assume you knew the ingredients all along. You will
soon appear to be a major *bon vivant,* if you do as we suggest!

Wine

Traditionally, wine is served with any nice meal. You need to
be ready to serve your guests wine, even if you are not a drinker
yourself. There are many types of wine, but the main categories
are White, Red, Blush, Dessert, and of course Champagne, which
is in a category all its own.

White Wine

White wine is generally served with fish or pasta, or any sub-
tly flavored food. The most common types of white wine include
Chardonnay, Sauvignon Blanc, Chenin Blanc, Pinot Grigio and
Johannisberg Riesling. Good California Chardonnays are Cha-
teau Montelena, Jordan Vineyard or Mayacamas. Good French
white wines are the Domaine Blain-Gagnard Chassagne-
Montrachet, Maison Louis Jadot, Puligny–Montrachet, or
Meursault. A good German white wine is Ockfenner Bockstein
and for the most part the German Reislings are excellent. For a
good bottle of white wine you will have to pay between twenty-
five and forty-five dollars.

Red Wine

Red wine is traditionally served with meat dishes or strongly
flavored food. The most common red wines are Cabernet
Sauvignons such as, Merlot, Zinfandel, and Pinot Noir. The
French Bourdeax are very good, as are upscale California red,
such as the Silverado Red. Opus One is also a very good red

wine, as are the Italian reds such as, Ruffino Gold Label, the Villa Antinori Chiannti and the Tignanello. You can expect to spend between thirty and fifty dollars for a good bottle of red wine.

Blush Wine

Blush wines are white wines made from red grapes. The most popular blush wine is a white zinfandel. Blush wines are much sweeter than whites. However, it could be considered unsophisticated and pedestrian to serve a blush wine, so avoid this category when trying to impress your target.

Dessert Wines

Dessert wines are much stronger in alcohol content than red or white wines (20 percent alcohol versus 13 percent, roughly). The dessert wines are usually sherry, such as Harvey's, Croft or Sandeman, or port such as Fonseca's, Taylor and Dow.

Champagne

Lastly there is champagne, or sparkling wine. If your sparkling wine does not come from the Champagne region of France, it is not champagne—it is sparkling wine. However, it is always a nice touch to have either champagne or high end sparkling wine available for serving. The best quality champagne for the money is **Charles Heidsieck**. For unforgetable occasions or to create a special impression, consider ordering **Champagne Krug**. This is the champagne of choice for the connoisseur and the fashionable crowd. For those on a tight budget, try the high end California sparkling wine **Shramasberg** or **Piper Sonoma**. Both are of good quality at a reasonable price.

If you are trying to impress someone who enjoys the James Bond movies, order Bolinger. It is the sparkling wine of choice for Mr. Bond.

The French conqueror Napoleon Bonaparte drank Möet & Chandon before every battle, with the exception of Waterloo. (Perhaps he should have sent someone out to the liquor store before that one.) In addition, Napoleon used to say that every time he won a battle he *deserved* a good bottle of champagne, and every time he lost one—he *needed* a good bottle of champagne!

Hard Liquor

Are you ready to be a bartender? The key to being a good bartender is knowing how to make drinks. Luckily for you, in *Appendix A* at the back of this book there is a list of over two hundred recipes for just about every mixed drink you are likely to ever be asked to make. Armed with this information, most of the battle to be a good and savvy host is won. Here is an over-view of the various drink categories.

The first category of hard liquor we will look at is **Bourbon** drinks. The most famous include Bourbon Collins, Bourbon Slow Gin Fizz, and the Mint Julep.

The next liquor category is **Brandy**. Mixed drinks that in-volve brandy include many fruit orientated drinks such as, Apri-cot Fizz, Apricot Cocktail, and Bossa Nova.

Cognac drinks include the Almond Frost, Alexander's Sis-ter, the Side Car and the Betsy Ross Cocktail.

Some of the more fun mixed drinks come from the **Liqueur** category. Drinks such as, an Amaretto Sour, Fuzzy Navel, Sex on the Beach, and a Sloe Gin Fizz come from cordials and li-queurs.

The next category is **Gin**, which is the basis for some of the most famous mixed drinks, including, the Gimlet, Gin Fizz, Long Island Iced Tea, Tom Collins and the classic Martini. Some fun Gin based drinks are the Singapore Sling, the Adios Mother, and ZuZu's Petals.

Famous **Rum** drinks include the Bahama Mama, The Blue Hawaiian, the Daiquiri, Mai Tai, and the Pina Colada.

In the **Scotch** family there is the Dry Rob Roy and the Rusty Nail.

Tequila is the main ingredient for the Tequila Sunrise and the Margarita.

From **Vodka** we get a number of famous drinks, including the Martini, Cosmopolitan, Seabreeze, Bloody Mary, Grey-hound, Harvey Wallbanger, Kamikaze, Screwdriver, and the White Russian.

Rounding out our hard liquor categories is **Whiskey**, whose drinks include the Highball, Manhattan, Boilermaker, and Whiskey Sour.

Make sure to use the Appendix in the back for drink recipes and you will be sure to impress your guests with your stunning and knowledgeable bartending skills.

Cigars

Can you truly be a great host these days without being able to provide a nice cigar after dinner? Probably not, especially if you are intent on Shmoozing your guest. If they are knowledgeable about cigars, they will certainly appreciate your interest. And if they are ignorant about cigars they will learn something about the subject and recognize your great wisdom on this mysterious new trend. Either way, you come up a winner when you learn to talk the talk about the hot subject of cigars.

Cigars have become the newest rage and are seen in the hands of celebrities, politicians, business tycoons, and the up-and-coming. Armed with a little knowledge about cigars, a few key accessories and a box of cigars, you can create an immediate impression of being on the cutting edge of today's style. What follows will give you the cigar knowledge you need to become a cigar aficionado and to hold your own in a cigar conversation. You will also learn valuable tips on choosing your accessories. In Appendix B, you will find a list of cigars arranged by manufacturer which will help you with your cigar shmoozing and purchases.

Let's begin at the beginning! Cigars are classified by a number of characteristics: ring gauge, length, wrapper, and tobacco origin. The **ring gauge** refers to the thickness of the cigar. The ring gauge is expressed in $1/64^{ths}$ of an inch. So if a cigar has a ring gauge of 64, it is 1 inch thick, or if the cigar has a ring gauge of 50, it is $50/64^{ths}$ of an inch wide.

The **length** of a cigar is expressed in inches, and cigar manufacturers generally name their cigars based on the length of the cigar. The most common cigar sizes (the exact size varies between cigar manufacturers) are the Robusto (5 inch, 50 ring), Corona

(5 ½ inch, 42 ring), Lonsdale (6 ½ inch, 42 ring), Churchill (7 inch, 48 ring), and Presidente (8 inch, 50 ring).

The cigar **wrapper** refers to the color of the cigar. The most common wrappers are natural, Connecticut, and Maduro. The Connecticut wrapper is very light, the Maduro very dark, and natural is the typical cigar color. There are a number of variations and subtle wrapper differences, but if you can recognize these three, you will be correct when you try and guess the wrapper 95% of the time.

The last of our cigar classifications is the cigar's **origin**. Cuban cigars are the most famous, however, they are illegal in the United States due to the embargo the U.S. currently has against Cuba. Other big cigar producing countries are the Dominican Republic, Honduras, Nicaragua, U.S.A., Mexico, and the Canary Islands.

So, if you know the cigar wrapper, the origin of the cigar, and the common sizes, you can basically carry yourself pretty well in a cigar conversation. You can always refer to Appendix B in the back of this book to help you with your actual cigar selection and you will be up to speed and set to order.

The only items left to concern yourself with are your **accessories**. You need to store the cigar, cut it, light it, and have someplace to put the ashes.

It is easy to pick out an ashtray, just get one that matches the decor of your home. It is a little more complicated to store your cigars. They must be kept in a moist environment. The typical way to store cigars is in a humidor. It is a wooden box that is close to airtight and lined with cedar. A small humidification device is attached to the inside and the cigars are kept fresh. You can purchase a humidor in a wide range of prices, from about $50 up to tens of thousands. If you are just beginning, look for a humidor that can hold about a hundred cigars and is not too fancy. You can purchase a nice one in this category for about $100. If you really want go about storing your cigars inexpensively, you can put them in Tupperware and store them in your refrigerator. This is not the best way and your cigars will eventually become stale, but it will keep the cigars for a while. This is not something you want to admit you do when you are out Shmoozing about cigars, trying to sound suave, savvy and knowledgeable!

To smoke a cigar, you first need to cut the end of the cigar so you can draw the smoke through it. You can use one of many types of cutters. There is the punch, which puts a hole in the end of the cigar; there is the cutter, which slices the end off of the cigar, and there is the v-wedge cutters which cut a small wedge into the end. You can purchase cutters for as little as five dollars, but I have also seen a gold cutter that sold for $2,500. Shop around and find one in your budget. Most cigar smokers prefer the guillotine cutter the best as it gives the smoker the smoothest draw without concentrating the tar from the tobacco into a small opening.

Finally, you need to light the cigar. You can use wooden matches or purchase a cigar lighter. I prefer the cigar lighter because it can help start a conversation if your lighter has some style, and conversations mean opportunities to Shmooze. Currently the Blazer is the most popular cigar lighter. You can pick up the futuristic Blazer for about $60. Another excellent lighter is the Colibri. The Colibri run about $100 but are beautiful and become instant conversation pieces, which can definitely help light up your Shmoozing activities.

When you light a cigar, begin by holding the cigar horizontal to the ground and slowly turn the end in the flame. Once you have heated the entire end put the cigar in your mouth and point the cigar down, towards the flame, at about a 45 degree angle. Slowly turn the cigar to light the entire end evenly. Once the cigar is lit, blow on the glowing end to ensure it is fully lit.

When choosing a cigar to impress people, you are safe to follow two theories. First, bigger is better. Buy large cigars. They look more expensive, and they seem more substantive. Second, you can never go wrong with the big four of cigars: Cohiba, Montecristo, Regalos, and Fuente Opus X. Of the four, Regalos might be your best bet, as they are more readily available and more reasonably priced. If you want a selection of cigars to offer, or want to try a different brand, at the end of this chapter we've provided a description of worthwhile cigars.

When trying to look like a cigar expert, it helps to be able to rate a cigar after smoking it. The good part is that cigar ratings generally are easy to make up, even if you have no idea what you are looking for, or cannot tell the difference between an expensive Cuban cigar and a cheap machine made cigar. The key is in the buzzwords. Below is a listing of typical cigar lingo and popular cigar adjectives. Merely fill in the following sample "Cigar Rating With Comments" sentence with the suggested adjectives. This will enable you to impress anyone who is listening, even the most ardent cigar aficionado. With a little practice, your cigar Shmooze will be impeccable.

Sample Cigar Rating With Comments:

The cigar seemed to me to be a beautifully crafted stick. Overall it was _____. The smoke had a hint of _____ and _____, with a _____ tone left on the palate. The finish was _____. This is a good after dinner cigar, or after any big meal.

"Overall" Adjectives: Well-balanced; Smooth tasting; Consistent; Has Herbal characteristics.
"Smoke" Adjectives: Mild nut; Coffee; Cocoa Bean; Orange (Peel); Hazelnut; Toasty spice; Cedar; Sweet Spice.
"Tone" Adjectives: Clean; Fresh; Mild; Earthy
"Finish" Adjectives: Consistent; Earthy; Strong; Sweet Spicy

As an example, here is a finished cigar rating with comments using the categories we've prepared for you:

"The cigar seemed to me to be a beautifully crafted stick. Overall it was <u>well-balanced</u>. The smoke had a hint of <u>mild nut</u> and <u>coffee bean</u>, with an <u>earthy</u> tone left on the palate. The finish was <u>strong</u>. This is a good after dinner cigar, or after any big meal."

You will sound like you are an expert in cigars and well-versed in the subtleties of cigar smoking. The interesting part of this Shmooze is that there are not many people who could argue with your assessment, as it takes years to develop a palate that can taste these subtle differences. And even then, the subtleties are so faint that it is tough to argue with another person's rating and observations. If you deliver this Shmooze with conviction you will wow all of your targets into submission.

Additionally, we've provided a handy reference chart of each cigar and its country of origin in Appendix B. You should briefly scan this list to familiarize yourself with the broad universe of cigars that are out there. Memorizing several of these could also be helpful to you when Shmoozing with the few truly knowledgeable cigar *aficionados* that are out there.

Recap

So, if you followed our advice: the house is clean, looks good, smells nice—the dinner is home made (at least the main course), you served a nice wine and/or champagne with the meal and offered after dinner mixed drinks, and the cigars were a big hit!

Do not forget to use your basic Shmooze skills discussed in the first two chapters to win your chosen guests over with your scintillating personality. These Shmooze techniques are all very effective, but you do not need to rely on them exclusively.

Remember to make an effort to be fun, dynamic, and interesting and always concentrate on the interests of your guests.

You're on your way to becoming a master Shmoozer!

6

HOW TO GET A JOB

This book has so far taught you how to make positive impressions, how to be the life of every party, and how to impress people. Let us now learn how to use these important skills to make some money.

We all know that when a company puts an ad in the paper advertising a decent job, they receive hundreds of resumés back from hopeful job seekers. This chapter will help to make you stand out and Shmooze your way to the job you want.

Resumés

Your job hunt will always start with resumés. Put together the best resumé you can that highlights your strengths. Begin the resumé with a profile section that summarizes your skills. Be very sure to custom tailor the profile section to the job you are try-ing for. Use the buzzwords that the employer used in its ad in your resumé's profile section. If the ad says they are looking for a self-starter, include a line in your profile section that says some-thing like, "I am a fast learner who is very motivated and action orientated." Enough cannot be said for customizing the profile section for your job search. You want to customize your resumé so you appear to be the perfect candidate. The key thing to un-derstand here is that you never want to let the resumé slow you down from getting a job. Do everything you can on that piece of paper to get your foot in the door. Once you are in, you know your Shmoozing skills will go a long way toward getting you the job you are seeking. But first you must make your resumé work to open the door for you.

Follow up the profile section with a chronological job list showing your responsibilities and significant achievements in your past positions. Here again, tailor your past responsibilities and job highlights towards the job you are going after. If you were a fry cook at McDonalds and you are going for a creative job at an ad agency, include in your responsibilities something similar to this: "Focused on customer perceptions in preparing final food presentations. Very motivated in winning customer sales and satisfaction through creative and innovative presenta-tion of product."

Every line in your resumé should be custom written to get the specific job you are after. In most cases, you should rework your resumé for each different job you are seeking.

Tips For Success:

When you send your resumés out, send them in a large 9" by 12" envelope. This way it will arrive unfolded, and thus will appear neater and more professional than those resumés folded into stan-dard small envelopes. Additionally, your large envelope will stand out from the usual pack of replies the company receives.

Another trick is to put your resumé in a personal size enve-lope in a non-traditional color. Hand address this envelope and send it directly to the decision maker. Typically whoever screens the mail for the decision maker will assume your Hallmark-looking envelope is a personal letter and they will send it right in to the boss unopened. Your resumé will then make it to the correct desk.

This latter method worked for Steve and I recently. We wanted to get a meeting with Les Moonves, the President of CBS television. We were having trouble getting past his very protective secretary, so we sent a letter with a short synopsis of our television concept and a request for a meeting, discreetly in a Hallmark card envelope. Sure enough, the personal-looking envelope was shuttled right to his desk and we finally cut through the bureaucracy and those running interference for him and we got our meeting. At the end of the meeting we asked him how he liked the technique we had used with the Hallmark envelope and he chuckled. He admitted that he had personally opened the envelope and mentioned that he had never been sent a request that way before. He also told us that he imagined this little trick of ours was so clever it would work every time!

Steve with CBS President Les Moonves (At a fundraiser at universal Studios).

Getting to the Right Person

It also helps when trying to get a job to be sure you are dealing with the right person. Typically, when an ad shows up in the paper, you are instructed to send your resumé back to the personnel office. You can gain a serious advantage over your competition if you are able to get directly in touch with the actual decision maker.

Do some homework and use the telephone to find out who will ultimately be doing the hiring. Let us assume that you are trying to get a job as a programmer at a computer company. To find the right person, call the main number of the company and ask who the vice president of development is. When you are told the vice president is Jill Hillion, thank the receptionist and hang up. Do not ask for Ms. Hillion during the initial call or you will probably be turned down. The receptionist will ask who you are and will inevitably warn the vice president that you just called and did not know her, before the call is transferred. Instead, you should call back a half hour later and ask for Jill Hillion. You will most likely be transferred without a problem. When you get the vice president on the phone be polite and just mention that you applied for the job they are hiring for and you wanted to express your sincere interest in the job and that you are looking forward to the interview at her convenience. Use your basic Shmooze skills to keep the conversation going, and try to create some positive moments. Once you have the decision maker on your side, or at least somewhat interested, the interview is yours and the job is that much closer. If you sense during the call that the person is too busy to Shmooze with you, it is always best for you to politely end the call, rather than have the hiring person try to get rid of you.

The Interview

Your resumé worked and you are now looking across the desk at your prospective employer. First and foremost, stay cool and collected. Remember a key tip in the basic Shmooze chapter—be confident. There is no reason why you should not get the job. They have called you in because they need someone like you to fill the position. With your Shmooze skills, who could beat you in an interview?

But just to be sure, let me provide you with some extra Shmoozing techniques that work magnificently in an interview. First of all, spend as much time discussing non-work issues as you can. The interviewer will usually begin the conversation with some type of ice-breaker—a little chit chat to see what type of a person you are and what sort of people skills you have. Play this part of the game up early in the interview. However, do not dwell on extraneous issues for too long. Get down to business and get some of the basics out of the way. Listen closely to the interviewer and answer his or her questions completely and as creatively as you can. Show him or her you are a thinker. When you get the feeling that you have discussed your qualifications and the position enough, try to smoothly change the subject. Use a transition from a business related answer into something personal. As an example, a couple of months back Steve and I were interviewing with a firm that wanted help launching a national marketing campaign for a new product. We spent some time discussing both our connections in the field and our marketing ideas to create a huge splash in their marketplace. We started discussing how we could use celebrities to help increase product awareness. I then transitioned the discussion to show the interviewer our personal celebrity picture album, which has thousands of shots of us with every major celebrity imaginable. The next hour was spent answering the interviewer's questions about our adventures and telling celebrity stories while the interviewer sat fascinated by page after page of our pictures. We knew that once we got the interviewer discussing celebrities, or anything that was non-business related, the marketing job was going to be ours. As predicted, we got the job and helped the firm successfully launch their product using our contacts with celebrities.

You too can use this transition technique in many different ways to your benefit. For instance, if you notice the interviewer has a golf-related paper weight, answer a question with a golf analogy and then end the answer by transitioning with a question about whether or not the interviewer plays golf. If you get an affirmative answer, you can be off and running on a non-business topic dear to the interviewer's heart and you will find yourself bonding quickly with the decision maker. Bonding. Connecting. Networking. Shmoozing. Call it what you want, you are using subtle techniques to improve your chances of getting the job.

Bad Interview, Good Interview

In the basic Shmooze chapter, I discussed how important buzzwords can be. This technique can be equally important during a job search. Let us assume you are a salesman. You have been selling walkie talkies for three years and you know it is time for you to move on. You see an ad for a job that sounds terrific, but it is selling telephone service with Sprint and you do not know the industry at all. The trick in this circumstance is to interview with some other company in the industry you are uncertain about, first. Make an appointment to go in and discuss job openings over at MCI. Get the practice interview (the bad interview where you do not really care what they think of you) out of the way by asking every question you can possibly imagine about the industry. Ask about sales cycles, sales strategies, the competition, how business is this year, etc. By the end of the interview there should be no ambiguity in your mind about how the industry works and how salesmen in the industry sell. Do not worry about giving the impression to the interviewer that you are a neophyte—you are! You are simply using the bad interview technique to learn about the industry. Now when your interview with Sprint comes along, you are an old pro. Get in there and Shmooze them like the professional you know you can be. The job is yours!

7

HOW TO SHMOOZE
AT PARTIES

You are at a major party and it is time to work the room. The previous chapters have given you the tools you need to handle yourself one-on-one with anyone. You can handle yourself in a savvy manner and Shmooze with the best of them. You even know a number of MAIs (Make An Impression) such as: pool shots, magic tricks, cigar chatter, and a wealth of Shmoozing tips & techniques you have learned up to this point. So at a party you can unleash yourself and be sure that you will make a serious impression with your Shmoozing skills. But what extra strategy can you apply when you are Shmoozing at parties to make your evening that much more valuable? The answer is volume. By this we mean you should maximize your Shmoozing potential by approaching as many people who look interesting as is possible. This book has demonstrated methods to Shmooze anyone. Now let us see how you can Shmooze everyone.

If you are going to take the time to attend a party and Shmooze, you might as well leave a strong impression—on just about everybody. We're serious!

The Priority List

Plan your rounds at a party by determining your priority list. If there is someone you really want to meet, then by all means go there first. Use your newly learned techniques such as the "pretend friend introduction" (see chapter two) as well as the rest of the basic Shmooze methods, to conquer all who are on your priority hit list.

So, let us say that there are one hundred people at a party. You have successfully Shmoozed the twelve people who were your targets at the party, and it is time to deal with the other eighty-eight. How do you decide where to go next? The best move is to go and talk to anyone who is standing around by themselves. They are dying to talk to someone and your Shmooze will receive a good reception, making your job easier. Next, go after groups of two people who are doing a lot of looking around the room. These are preferably members of the opposite sex so you can possibly add them to your future dating list or refer them to your friends. (We consider referrals to friends as very important because you generate good will from both your friends and from the people you have just Shmoozed. We call this "recycling"). Probably the only people these two know at the party are each other, so again, your opening line, and Shmooze techniques will be well received and easy to work. And, your targets will probably be thankful for the attention. Next, approach the largest groups. You can use your Shmooze to bond with many people at once. If the party is larger, you can save a lot of time this way. The last groups you want to approach, if you bother with them at all, are couples that seem to be romantic. They probably do not want to be interrupted and they most likely have little to offer you, so consider passing on them, unless you see some tell-tale signs that the couple may not be happy together which means there could be a reason for you to move in for a Shmooze attempt on the member of the couple you are interested in. If you see the guy checking out other women, he probably is not that interested in the girl he appears to be coupled with. Watch his eyes as attractive girls pass him and see if they dart after them. You can assume that either party in this couple is a good candidate for your Shmooze. And if you spot a couple where the woman is flirting aggressively with single guys in the room, you can assume either party in this couple is also fair game for Shmoozing. Don't be shy. Remember, **those who are shy, are lost!**

If you really want to Shmooze with a couple that seem happy together, a good trick in this situation is to act like the host of the party and just discreetly butt in to their conversation and say that you just want to make sure everything is going well, and you wanted to see if they needed a new drink or anything. Now do not get us wrong. We are not advocating that you lie about being the host. But if you walk up to a couple and ask if everything is going all right and if they need a new drink, the impression is that you are the host or at least helping the host. It is an easy opening line, and is non-intrusive to these romantic couples. By the way, if they say they do need a new drink, you should quickly point in the direction of the bar and politely tell them there is plenty of alcohol left, then smile and quickly move on. Do not get caught up getting drinks for people—you are not a waiter! You are a Shmoozer! You are on a mission!

You may wonder why we advocate that you should try to talk to everyone. The answer is: Because they are there and they may be interesting, fun, exciting, or a valuable resource. Additionally if you are a single guy or girl, isn't meeting good, new people what it is all about? Won't you have a better chance of becoming friends with appropriate new people if you are out actively hunting for them? Do you think your ideal mate is going to just find you if you don't help the situation along? Prince Charming is not there looking for you, you've got to find him. And Miss Right is certainly not going to find your sorry ass if you don't go out and hunt for her. You've got to go out there and give them some reason to want to go out with you and find out how terrific you are. This means you've got to boldly and effectively Shmooze your way into a date with her or him!

So, these are the reasons why you should consider meeting everyone in a party!

Timing is Everything

It is quite a challenge to find time to Shmooze everyone at a party. One problem that crops up is when you unfortunately approach someone who is desperate for a conversation or looking for a new best friend. If your target takes a liking to you, they might prefer to be with you and they may not want to talk to anyone else at the party. When you encounter this sort of needy person who wants to monopolize too much of your time, you have got to quickly get yourself out of this situation. There are a number of graceful ways to exit these conversations.

The first way is the simple "I need to get a drink", or "I need to use the facilities" line. It is tough for someone to deny you when you are thirsty or you need to go to the bathroom. And when you leave under these circumstances, the time-wasting person doesn't get angry at you. So use the line, head in the direction of the bar or bathroom, and presto, you are free.

The next way to extricate yourself is to suddenly "remember" that you promised to help the host or hostess with something.

Or, you can keep your tag along happy by telling them you need to mingle, but offer to bring them along. They will be delighted. Then you must deftly get them involved in the conversation with the next group you approach, and then discreetly leave them with their new found friends. They will probably latch on to them as aggressively as they did to you, allowing you to politely exit, moving on to more productive conversations.

A Few Smart Tips on Dressing

1. If you are a tall man, do not wear stripes, you'll just seem even bigger.

2. If you are a short man, do not wear a sportcoat with different color pants. The color cuts you off in the middle and makes you appear even shorter.

3. At night, men should wear darker colors. (Hey, our society today thinks this is a cool look. Don't blame us if you don't want to be a "boy-in-black". Blame the fashionistas who start these crazy trends!)

4. Do not overdo it on the jewelry. Be tasteful and wear jewelry appropriate for where you will be. Long jingling earrings don't cut it at the office if you want to be taken seriously.

5. Always try to dress to impress, but be appropriate for the location and crowd you are with.

6. The Miami Vice look is over. Dress for this decade.

7. When all else fails, men wear Hugo Boss or Armani, women wear Donna Karan or Calvin Klein. These designers are tasteful, classic and always in style.

8. Always have nice polished shoes. You could be wearing a great suit, but if the shoes are scuffed people will notice and you will have blown the whole great impression. Oh, yea, make sure your socks match.

9. The same shoe advice holds for women, with the addition of the handbag. You are better off with a simple outfit and nice accessories, than to show up with worn out shoes or a mismatched handbag.

10. When in doubt, dress up, do not dress down. You can always turn an over-dressed outfit into a more casual look, but you can not easily take casual and dress it up.

CAUTION

Be careful who you listen to for fashion advice. You are reading our opinions, but first you might want to check out our homely pictures throughout this book and the clothes we are wearing. We are not far from Mr. Blackwell's worst dressed list. We tend to be fashion misfits, but we do try to follow this same simple advice we're giving you. You should, too.

8

HOW TO SHMOOZE
AT BARS/CLUBS

When you go out to bars and clubs, you will either hang out with your friends, or try to meet new, interesting people. Now that you've studied the advice in this book, you should never only hang out with your friends. You can use your Shmooze techniques to guarantee yourself a good time and a successful evening. Go for it! Remember to use your conversational Shmooze techniques such as: eye contact, interest in your target's topics, using your target's first name, and all the others. Also, very important in a club setting is how you begin your conversation. The best approach is to be confident and be yourself. Go up and introduce yourself, or use the "pretend friend introduction" (see Chapter 2 "Shmooze Basics") to begin a conversation.

You can also try one of the several "pick-up lines" which we've identified below. While many of these lines could get you slapped, as opposed to getting a conversation going, most of them are at least extremely humorous and will generate smiles, if nothing else. People love humor and funny people. If you deliver these lines as if what you're saying is supposed to be humorous, there is a good chance these openers will work. We have personally used a lot of these lines and we've seen them actually work in bar, party and social settings. The most important thing is to deliver them while smiling kindly and sincerely to the intended target. You should be able to evoke a laugh or a giggle from most of these lines and then you should deftly shift the conversation to introducing yourself and your associate, if are working as a team, and try to get a real conversation going. Once there is the initial give and take between you and the ice is broken, the time is right to begin dazzling your target with your Shmoozing abilities.

If you sense the person was very shocked by your irreverent comments, a quick, "I'm just kidding!" or "I'm just making a joke!" accompanied by a nice smile will alleviate the tension and hopefully allow you to gain the entry you need to get further conversation and a good Shmooze going.

It is always helpful to have some sort of plan on what you will do, assuming you're successful and do get a lively conversation going with your intended target. You should have a few suggestions on where you both might go afterwards: a nearby bar, ice cream parlor, place for dinner or desert, etc. In addition, you should have a plausible reason to exchange numbers with your target, such as: a party you are soon throwing (or your friends are soon having) that you would like to invite the target and their friends to, a cool upcoming event, such as; a concert, museum opening, charity party, black tie benefit, theater, etc.; or just dinner and a movie. This enticement to invite the new found friend to something social will help you gauge their level of interest in you. It will also give them an excuse to do what they subliminally want to do—which is to give you their card or phone number so you have a way of following up with them in the future. The key is to give your target the right excuse to give you their phone number! If they enthusiastically give up their card or number, you can be sure there is some level of interest. Maybe it is just curiosity or interest in your party and not you, but successfully getting their number so you can talk to them a second time and you can attempt to convince them to meet with you or to attend a function with you in the future, gives you many additional Shmoozing options to pursue with that person.

Smart Shmoozers will recognize that when meeting new members of the opposite sex, if there is not a mutual attraction initially, there are still many beneficial things that can come from the new encounter. For instance, the person may not be attracted to you in the beginning, but if you keep in touch with them and they see you in different situations, they might eventually come to realize what a good person you truly are. Alternatively, you can refer this person to your friends, which will give you Shmoozing points with both your friends and with the intended target. This becomes a win-win situation for you. (This activity was referred to previously by its technical term, "recycling"). And finally, the person may meet and date your friends, but realize that you are the real prize and come around to wanting to be with you after all. Because you handled yourself smartly and respectfully from the beginning and didn't chase a losing proposition, you may end up with that person in the end, and receive all the Shmoozing benefits along the way. Not a bad outcome. All it takes is a savvy, patient, and smart Shmooze approach.

Good luck with your Shmoozing and these following introduction lines. Remember, deliver them with a smile and some panache!

Suggested Humorous Introductory Lines
Use only the ones that you would be comfortable saying.

A. Flirtatious Lines

1. Excuse me, can I flirt with you?

2. Bring a chair with you over to your target and smile while asking, "Is this seat taken?" Then put the chair down and sit on it and start talking.

3. Do you have a girlfriend/boyfriend? [No.] Are you taking applications?

4. You see my friend over there? [Point to friend who sheepishly waves from afar] He wants to know if YOU think I'M cute.

5. You look like a girl who has heard every single line in the book—so what's one more sincere line from me!

6. Were your parents Greek gods? Because it takes two gods to make a goddess.

7. Were you ever in the Boy Scouts? Because you sure have tied my heart in a knot!

8. Was it love at first sight, or should I walk by again?

9. Pardon me miss, I seem to have lost my phone number. Could I borrow yours?

10. Nice to meet you, I'm (your name) and you are...Gorgeous!

11. (Look at the tag on her shirt and say) "I wanted to see if you were really made in heaven."

12. It seems as if I'm in a fairy tale. {"Why?"} Because I see a beautiful princess standing right in front of me.

13. Is your father a thief? Because he stole the stars from the skies and put them in your eyes!

14. Is there an airport nearby or is that just my heart taking off?

15. Is it hot in here? Or is it just you?

16. If your parents hadn't met I'd be very a very unhappy man right now!

17. If I follow you home, will you keep me?

18. I'm in the process of writing a telephone book. May I have your number?

19. I was sitting here holding this bottle (or glass) and I realized I'd rather be holding you.

20. I hope you know CPR, cuz you take my breath away!

21. I am a student of love. Here's my card.

22. Hi, we're taking a survey and I need your phone number. If you give it to me, I'll call you and tell you the results.

23. Hi, my name is {name}. How do you like me so far?

24. Hi, can I buy you a car?

25. Hey, weren't you Miss Virginia last year?

26. Hey, don't I know you? Yeah, you're the girl with the beautiful smile!

27. Have you seen (any movie)? Would you like to?

28. Have you always been this cute, or did you have to work at it?

29. Excuse me. I haven't met you yet and I have to leave soon. My name is _____. What's yours?

30. Your warm eyes melt the iciness of my lonely heart.

31. Excuse me, but I've had a pretty bad day, and it usually makes me feel better to see a pretty girl smile. So, would you please smile for me?

32. Excuse me, but I think I dropped something!!! MY JAW!!

33. Excuse me, but where have you been all my life?

34. Do you have a passport? (YES) Good, I want to take you shopping.

35. Do you have a map? I just get lost in your eyes.

36. You: Excuse me, were you talking to me?
    Her: No.
    You: Well then, please start!

37. Could you please stand still so I can have a chance to pick you up!

38. Can you live happily on 4,000 a month?

39. Can I have directions? (To where?) To your heart!

40. Can I call an ambulance? [Why?] When I saw you my heart stopped!

41. Can I borrow a quarter? Cause my mom told me to call home when I met the girl of my dreams.

42. You're cuter than a speckled pup.

43. Baby, somebody better call God, 'cuz he's missing an angel!

44. Are you religious? 'Cause I'm the answer to all your prayers!

45. Are you OK? Because Heaven's a long fall from here.

46. Are you lost ma'am? Because obviously you came from heaven and that's a long way from here.

47. Am I dead? We are in heaven, aren't we? You obviously are one of God's angels, aren't you?

48. (Checking her shirt tag) Excuse me, I was just making sure you were the right size!

49. (With hands on her shoulder bladess) Oh, those are shoulder blades? I thought they were Angel's wings!

B. Politically Incorrect Lines. (Use with caution!)

Women can study the "Suggested Humorous Rebuttals" at the end of this section for use when they hear these sorts of lines.

50. Would you like to have breakfast tomorrow? Should I nudge you—or call you?

51. Would you like Gin and platonic, or would you prefer Scotch and sofa?

52. I'm new in town, could I get directions to your place?

53. What would you do if I couldn't restrain myself any longer and kissed you right now?

54. Walk up to a lady you are interested in at a social gathering (party, club, dinner, etc.) and smile and a simply ask in your most charming voice, "Are you ready to go home now?"

55. That's a nice shirt...could I talk you out of it?

56. That dress just looks great on you...as a matter of fact, so would I. [This one's dangerous no matter how you say it.]

57. She: (to passing man) Do you have the time?
    Him: (smiling) Do you have the energy?

58. My lenses turn dark in the sunshine of your love.

59. May I please rest my head on your shoulder?

60. Lie down please. I think I love you. [Dangerous].

61. If you were a tear in my eye I would not cry for fear of losing you.

62. If I told you that you had a beautiful body, would you hold it against me? [You could get a slap if this is delivered improperly!]

63. If I could rearrange the alphabet, I'd put U & I together.

64. I'm really sorry about Al. It was a lovely funeral we both attended. You look ravishing in black, did you know that? What you need now is a nice back rub. Are the straps too tight, darling? How tragic. How very, very tragic.

65. Who's a nice girl doing in a place like this?

66. I know a great way to burn off the calories from that pastry you just ate.

67. I can sense that you're a terrific lover, and it intimidates me a little.

68. How do you like your eggs cooked? (Why?) Well I just wanted know what to make for you in the morning!

69. Hi, the voices in my head told me to come talk to you!

70. Hey, didn't we go to different schools together?

71. Here's a quarter....call your roommate and tell her you won't be coming home tonight!

72. Her: What do you think of this (dress, sweater, blouse, etc.)
    Him: I like nothing...better.

73. Good looking waitress pouring a drink: Say when!
    Guy: As soon as I finish this drink!

74. Excuse me, but I'm a little short on cash, would you mind if we shared a cab to your place together?

75. Do you like music? (Yes) Good, I've got a great stereo in my car!

76. Do you know, your hair and my pillow are perfectly color coordinated?

77. Do you have a library card?, Cause I definitely wanna check you out!

78. Do you have a boyfriend? Well, when you want a MANfriend, come and talk to me.

79. Can I see your tan lines?

80. Are you looking for Mr. Right? Or Mr. Right Now?

81. Are you interested in finding Mr. Right? Or maybe just Mr. Maybe-He'll-Do-For-The-Night? [A little strong].

82. Are you from Tennessee? Because you are the only ten-I-see!

83. (While in the produce department) How can you tell if these things (cantalopes) are ripe?

84. (To a female at the copy machine) Reproducing, eh? Mind if I help?

Obviously, you should take many of these lines and just use them as jokes among your friends. But some selected ones do actually work and will assist you in getting some sort of an interchange and Shmooze going. Choose the ones you are comfortable with and memorize them for future use.

Once you are past the opening line, you will have hopefully broken the ice enough to begin an intelligent conversation and start your irresistible Shmooze.

Suggested Humorous Rebuttal Lines For Women and Men

OK, so you use a pick-up line and get rejected, or a pick-up line is used on you and you are insulted. Here is a quick look at the anti-Shmooze. No more making friends and Shmoozing the situation. Get some revenge! Here are some humorous lines that can be used to reject inappropriate pick-up lines.

1. **Pick-Up:** "Would you like to come back to my place?"
   Rejection: "Well, I don't know. Will two people fit under a rock?"

2. **Pick-Up:** "WOW! I'd really like to get into your pants."
   Rejection: "No thanks. There's already one ass in there!"

3. **Pick-Up:** "Haven't we met somewhere before?"
   Rejection: "Yes, I'm the receptionist at the V.D. Clinic."
   Rejection: (less politically correct) "Yes, I'm the Doctor at the AIDS Clinic."

4. **Pick-Up:** "I'd like to call you. What's your number?"
   Rejection: "It's in the phone book."
   Keep Trying: "But I don't know your name."
   Rejection: "That's in the phone book too.

5. **Pick-Up:** "So what do you do for a living?"
   Rejection: "I'm a Female impersonator."

6. **Pick-Up:** (From an older man) "Where have you been all of my life?"
   Rejection: "For the first half of it, I probably wasn't born yet."

7. You're walking down the street with a friend, and a member of the opposite sex walks by. Your friend watches the person go by, who takes offense at the looks she receive. She says, "What are you looking at?"
   Get some revenge with: "He thought you were good looking. Wow!! Was he mistaken!"

8. **Pick-Up:** "Hey, come on, we're both here at this bar for the same reason!"
   Rejection: "Yeah! Let's pick up some chicks!"

9. **General Rejection to lame Pick-Ups:** "Sorry, I don't date outside my species."

10. *Pick-Up:* "Would You Like to Dance?"
    Reply: "No, thank you."
    Revenge: "Don't thank me. Thank God somebody asked you!"

Bar Tricks that Attract Attention

If you are a person who is uncomfortable with using an opening line, you can use the following bar tricks to get people's attention focused on you. The tricks are easily performed and do not take any particular skill to successfully complete. Once your target begins watching you in action, you can't help but get a little Shmooze going, as you discuss the masterful bar trick that you had just performed. With minimal practice you can become an accomplished performer!

The Ford Fairlane

Put a little Sambuca in a glass and light the Sambuca on fire. Put your hand over the glass to extinguish the flame. The fire will burn off all of the oxygen and then go out. With no oxygen, a strong suction is created on your hand. You can then lift your hand and the glass will stick. Wave your hand around, and the glass will still not come off. Your target will think you're pretty sharp and you should be able to parlay this good will starting light conversation, thanks to this opener.

The Flying Coin

This is a pool trick you can successfully use at a bar. You can shoot the cue ball, hit a coin on the edge of the table, which will fling the coin straight up into the air, landing in a glass placed on the side of the pool table.

Put a quarter on the very edge of the table, on the felt. Set up a glass on the edge of the table, just past the quarter. Hit the cue ball from across the table directly at the coin and the glass.

With a little practice you will learn how hard to hit it. Once you get the speed, the coin will flip up and fall right in the glass. This impresses them every time and suddenly makes you a star!

Iron Thumbs

First, place a beer bottle on its side on the edge of a bar or table. Then challenge someone to lift the bottle into the air horizontally using only their two thumbs. No matter how strong they are, when they lift the bottle with their thumbs, the bottle is too heavy to lift horizontally, the base of the bottle will stay on the bar.

How it's Done:

You can perform this trick with a little technique, instead of brute force. Link the fingers of both hands, with your thumbs pointing away from you, approach the bottle from the narrow end. Now angle your thumbs downwards at 45 degrees. Grasp the neck of the bottle between your two thumbs, near the top of your thumbs (near your hand) and lift. Your linked figures give you enough leverage to use your thumbs as levers. The bottle will rise and you will reap the rewards from a satisfied audience of onlookers.

Slam Dunk Olive

Take a brandy glass and an olive and challenge someone to get the olive into the brandy glass without touching or smashing the olive. No one will be able to do this without prior knowledge of this trick.

Show them how it's done by putting the glass over the olive and then moving the glass in a fast circular motion. The centrifugal force will pull the olive up into the glass. Then quickly flip the glass over. Presto—the olive is in the glass! Your intended target is duly impressed.

Glass Handcuffs

The Set-Up:

Challenge a friend to balance a full glass of beer on the back of each of their hands. Get your friend to place both hands, palms down, on a bar. Then balance a full glass on the back of each hand. They, of course, will be able to balance the glasses, as this is not so difficult to do.

The fun:

Now, just smile and walk away while waving to them. They are now effectively "handcuffed" to the bar. They cannot move without spilling the beer and possibly breaking the glass, or without getting help.

Olympic Discus

The Challenge:

Bet your friend you can throw a bottle top twice as far as they can.

How it's Done:

Give your friend an ordinary bottle top and let them throw first. Then secretly hide a penny inside your bottle top by bending the edge over slightly. This gives extra weight and your bottle top will travel further. You're such a he-man!

When you go out on the town, relax and try to have a good time and good things will inevitably come your way.

How Long is Your Ash

With this technique you can smoke a cigarette completely down to the filter without the ash breaking off. You end up with a three inch ash perfectly in place.

How it's Done:

Take a cigarette from your pack, then straighten a paper clip until it is one long piece. Slide the paper clip into the middle of the cigarette until it is completely hidden inside the cigarette. When you smoke the cigarette, the straightened paper clip will keep the ash intact and long. No one will be able to see the paper clip, but the long ash will amaze everyone. You can perform this trick with a cigar as well. It wows them every time.

Magic Water

Pour a small amount of water into a saucer. Place an upturned glass into the center of the saucer. Bet someone you can get all of the water into the glass without tilting the saucer.

How it's Done:

Lift the glass off of the saucer. Bend a match at a right angle (90 degrees). Balance the match on the saucer with the top part pointing up. Use a quarter to anchor the bottom of the match on the saucer. Light the match and quickly replace the glass over the top of the lit match and coin.

A vacuum will be created by the match burning off the oxygen in the over-turned glass. The water will then be sucked into the glass. (You're now becoming a regular scientist.)

Pop Goes the Penny

Stand a cold empty beer bottle on a bar. Make sure the lip of the bottle is wet. Place a penny flatly on the wet rim of the bottle. Then announce that you can make the penny pop up at least three times without moving the bottle or touching or blowing the penny.

How it's Done:

With warm hands, grip the bottle tightly in a clasping fashion and wait. The temperature of your hands will warm the bottle, which will expand the air inside the bottle. This effect will eventually make the coin flip up at least three times, sometimes more depending on how cold the bottle is to start with. (You keep this up and soon you'll be giving David Copperfield some competition-and you know who he Shmoozed?)

Conclusion

If you mix fun, confidence and your Shmoozing techniques together you will have a terrifically successful time when you go out on the town. Relax and try to have a good time and good things will inevitably come your way.

9

GET WHAT YOU WANT THROUGH SHMOOZING

You will quickly discover that when you master the fine art of the Shmooze, you will be able to get exactly what you want more often than you would ever believe possible. When you are really "on" and your Shmooze is flowing, people can't help but respond. Your target will enjoy your company and be willing to do what they can to help you out.

You can just imagine all the situations where this can become valuable—getting upgraded to first class when you fly, getting your hotel rooms upgraded, getting seats at crowded restaurants, going backstage at concerts—any situation where a Shmooze target can personally help you—you'll get help, if you master the Shmooze.

Sometimes the one missing piece to getting something you want is asking for it. Use your Shmoozing techniques to put yourself in a position where the people you've Shmoozed can do something to help you out, but do not be shy and neglect to ask for their help. Here are a couple of specific examples:

Upgrading Your Airline Seat

The common perception when it comes to flying first class on an airline is that you have to either pay an exorbitant amount of money, or if you are a frequent flyer, use upgrade certificates. But there is an easier way. The agents working the counter to check you and your bags in have the ability to upgrade fliers to first class at their discretion on their orders. They are given this ability as a customer service tool to help appease service related situations and to generate good will for their airline.

Celebrities commonly are upgraded to first class, as are passengers that have been extremely inconvenienced due to a mistake caused by the airline. Use the power the agent has to upgrade people to first class by Shmoozing them to your advantage. Here's a scenario that works for us. You can probably come up with others that are just as good.

When you first walk up to the counter, start off with a line like, "You guys must be going nuts, this place is a zoo today!" The airport always seems like a zoo, and the agents always feel overworked, so this line is very successful and shows them that you care about how difficult their jobs are and you recognize how wonderful they are. Follow up the "You must be busy" conversation with either a simple question about your destination or a request for a recommendation for a dinner location, or how many gates the airline occupies at the destination airport, or how many hours straight do they have to work, etc. Agents love to talk about travel. Travel is their lives—that is why they work in the low paying industry of travel. The free travel they get as perks is their real motivation. During the conversation work in the agent's name a few times. Their name is on their tag so you don't have to be Sherlock Holmes. But you do have to be savvy and smooth and not obvious about what you are really up to, manipulation! Also concentrate on eye contact. Once you develop a bond with your Shmooze target, ask the question! Ask the agent if there is any way you can get bumped up to first class. You will be very surprised at how amenable the agent will be to this request. If there are seats available in first class, chances are, if your Shmooze was decent, you will be given one. Never underestimate your unlimited powers of persuasion!

I generally use an added trick to help cement the deal. I carry a small travel humidor for cigars. It is fairly unique looking. As I am checking in and Shmoozing the agent, I ask if he thinks it is a good idea for me to check my humidor in with the luggage. Invariably the agent will ask something about the cigars and then I, being the savvy gentleman Shmoozer that I am, graciously offer one of them. I never check in the humidor, but I can always steer the conversation around to my cigars without looking like I am trying to blatantly bribe the agent. Once the cigar is given, the agent is very thankful and usually puts me in first class without me even asking and gives me access to the first class waiting lounges. But in case the agent doesn't bring up the subject of an upgrade, I always do, and they are generally happy to comply, if there is room.

You can also use the Shmooze on the check-in person if your luggage is overweight. Once you've exchanged enough words to have bonded, you should then smile sweetly and ask if they could possibly help you out with your luggage as it might be a bit overweight. It is totally up to this person as to whether you get charged or not and if they like you, you can be sure you're not going to be paying any extra money!

Better Hotel Rooms

You can use the above airline techniques almost exactly the same way to get a better hotel room. Hotel clerks also have the power to upgrade your room to a suite. One trick that has been around for quite a long time is to tell the clerk it is your honeymoon and ask for an upgrade. Most hotels will upgrade a honeymoon couple, if a suite is available.

The "honeymoon couple" trick usually will work, but dishonesty is not really necessary. Use the Shmooze techniques to get a conversation going and then show some empathy for the hard work the clerk must get stuck doing when the long lines of pesky customers all check in or out at the same time. Once you create a friend—ask the question. When you ask for the room upgrade you will more often than not be accommodated if better rooms are available.

10

WHAT WORKS WITH THE PEOPLE AT THE TOP

During the process of putting together this book, Steve and I went to over one hundred celebrity events and asked some of the world's most famous people about their opinions on the subject of Shmoozing. We got very personal. We asked what kind of Shmoozing they did on a daily basis, what kind of Shmoozing they had to do to become successful, and what kind of Shmoozing works when used *on them?*

The answers were usually less than earth shattering. There were common threads that we noticed running through most of the answers. In response to our question on how the celebrities currently Shmooze people, they usually mentioned smiling and trying to appear happy during media interviews and public appearances. Even when they are in a bad mood, or just not up for the attention, they told us that they feel the constant need to put on their best face and pretend they are having a wonderful time. This technique goes back to what our book points out in a number of sections. In the "Shmooze at Work" chapter, we talk about being energetic and not complaining about workloads or how tired you might be. The parallel is definitely there between putting on the "I love my job" face and the celebrities putting on the "I love to do interviews" face.

When asked about what Shmoozing had to be done by the celebrity to "make it to the top," the typical response was "hard work". Most of the celebrities felt they had worked hard for their success and their Shmoozing consisted of getting themselves into the right place at the right time, and then creating friends who could become good contacts for them. It was interesting to observe the celebrities all saying that they wanted us to know that it was their "hard work" that got them to the top, but then they would go on to explain how networking and creating relationships put them in a position to allow their hard work to pay off. After hearing this rap many times, we realized that for a change we were being Shmoozed by the celebs!

Throughout this book, proven techniques have been provided to help you build a relationship quickly and effectively. Once you develop those relationships, you can use them to their fullest advantage. But be sure not to be just a user of people—relationships are built on two-way streets. If you want someone to help you out, be prepared to help them out. There is nothing wrong with getting help from a friend, but there is something wrong with abusing a friendship. If someone does something special for you, you should be thinking about something nice that you can do back for them, to thank them for their efforts on your behalf. Don't wait for someone to ask you for assistance in an area you know they need help in. If they are a friend, you should be constantly thinking about how you can help them.

The final category of questions for the celebrities was, "What works for those people who approach them and try to Shmooze with them?" We wanted to know—from the celebrities themselves—"What were the best techniques for approaching and Shmoozing a celebrity?"

The common themes here were honesty and being yourself. Almost to a person, the celebrities said they can spot someone being phony a mile away. They prefer someone to come up to them and be honest, and be themselves.

We think this assessment by the celebrities is a wish for the perfect world. We have found that celebrities are some of the easiest people to Shmooze. They spend so much time dealing with ardent admirers that when someone comes up and starts a non-show business related conversation, they are relieved and talk longer to you. This is a successful Shmooze technique, as we have explained previously to you. Steve and I always try to start conversations with celebrities on non-show business topics. This is not necessarily being ourselves or being honest. But we have an agenda which is to engage this celebrity in as interesting a conversation as is possible. That's because we are Shmoozers! We use the techniques explained in this book to help ensure that happens, and celebrities, for some odd reason, seem almost more susceptible to the techniques than other "more average" targets.

We appreciate the time the following celebrities gave us and thank them for their generous outpouring of thoughts on the subject of Shmoozing. We hope this information is helpful to your Shmoozing development.

MOVIE STARS' TRUE CONFESSIONS ON SHMOOZING

James Woods
John Travolta
Quentin Tarantino
Howard Stern
Sylvester Stallone
Kevin Spacey
Tim Robbins
Burt Reynolds
Brad Pitt
Joe Pesci
Bill Murray
Steve Martin

Samuel L. Jackson
Dennis Hopper
Bob Hope
Tom Hanks
Robert Downey Jr.
Danny DeVito
Johnny Depp
Willem Defoe
Jim Carrey
Tom Arnold
Kirstie Alley
Woody Allen

Bret with James Woods (At the American Television Awards).

James Woods

"I just like to have interesting conversations, so when people come up to me to Shmooze it's nice if we have common interests."

When we spoke with James about Shmoozing he reiterated a point we have made numerous times in this book: keep the conversation based around your subject's interests. James is saying that he enjoys conversations when they are interesting, and they will obviously be more interesting to him if you use our advice and discuss topics he finds entertaining.

Bret with John Travolta and John's wife, Kelly Preston (At the Oscar Awards).

John Travolta

"Keep in mind that anything is possible."

When we asked John about his feelings on using Shmoozing as a method of getting ahead in life, he gave us his upbeat view. This is a great attitude to live by. It pumps you up each day to keep thinking that *you can* achieve anything. If you do not limit yourself with negative thoughts, you can truly set out to accomplish anything. Once you decide something is impossible, it definitely becomes unattainable—for you. So, keep it positive and as John Travolta advocates, believe everything is attainable.

You can harness your Shmooze technique and use it as another tool to achieve what you are seeking in your life.

Bret with Quentin Tarantino (At the Emmy Awards).

Quentin Tarantino

"Have something to say when you're Shmoozing."

Quentin told us that he does not start a conversation with someone unless he feels he has something real to talk to the person about. That is easy advice for a guy who has a talent for writing dialog for a living. He always has something witty to say! But the advice is important.

Throughout this book we have given you methods and techniques to start and continue a conversation. You never want an awkward pause or a shallow question to destroy a positive moment. With our Shmoozing techniques you will not have this problem. However, you must use your judgement to make sure that you don't ask an inappropriate or boring question just so you have something to say to your targeted person. Take a few minutes, get your thoughts together, and come up with something relevant and intelligent to ask. Your question is a reflection on you—make sure there is a good chance for a positive result.

Howard Stern with Steve (At the Rainbow Room in New York City).

Howard Stern

"You guys are geniuses."

OK, so including this self-serving quote from Howard when we recently Shmoozed him was just an excuse to blow our own horn again. But Howard Stern is a terrific example of the human Shmooze machine. His controversial, intimate interviews use every Shmooze technique known to man. That is why he is so successful and why listeners love him over all his competition and numerous imitators.

We have met Howard on a dozen occasions and at every meeting he has been unbelievably cordial and giving of his time. On the air he can be the most sharpwitted, caustic and tyrannical talk show host, as he and his dysfunctional staff perform their daily entertaining shtick for millions of listeners—shocking us, amusing us and fascinating us with what he can get away with.

Howard Shmoozes about the most controversial topics, while mesmerizing listeners who can't believe what comes out of his mouth both on TV (*E-Entertainment Network*) and his internationally syndicated radio show. Thanks for entertaining us all with your unique Shmooze every morning! (And f-Jackie! But check out his new book: *Jackie "The Jokeman" Martling's Jokebook.*)

Sylvester Stallone with Bret (At a Planet Hollywood opening).

Sylvester Stallone

"Just be yourself and avoid being phony."

Stallone is an impressive presence wherever he is. We've met him numerous times at celebrity events and we've always noticed how well he uses humor and how articulate he is when answering questions. He told us that he prefers people to be sincere and not try some cute line on him. Celebrities can spot the phonies, the frauds, the opportunists, and the social climbers, miles away.

We'll remember Sly's advice the next time we're Shmoozing with him. You should also keep his advice in mind as it will serve you well to avoid being viewed as one of the negative types described above.

Bret with Kevin Spacey (At the Santa Monica Pediatric Aids Fund Raiser).

Kevin Spacey

"You guys know what works–have a good personality and have fun when you're Shmoozing."

Kevin is one of the most enjoyable celebrities to talk with. He is down to earth and makes you feel comfortable immediately. He also has identified a good point that no one else has made: Have a good personality when you are Shmoozing. This means be interesting, be dynamic, be intelligent and all of the other things associated with having a "good personality".

We have been lucky enough to meet Kevin a dozen times at various social events and have been able to use the Shmooze to strike up a friendship. By using the Shmoozing tips in this book you can do the same in your personal and work lives.

Bret with Tim Robbins (At the pre-party for the Oscar Awards).

Tim Robbins

"At the end of the day, true friends are all that matter."

This is certainly very good advice, however, you cannot have a true friend until you first meet him or her. And using these Shmoozing techniques puts you in the crucial position to make the friendships happen.

Tim's view on Shmoozing is that superficial friendships are not worth chasing. We agree with Tim, but we would add something more to his advice. Try to make new friends whenever possible. These Shmoozing techniques will allow you to meet as many new people as you like, many of whom will eventually turn into "true friends". Keep the true friends, spend minimal time with the superficial ones.

Burt Reynolds

"First ask yourself what's the worst thing that can happen. Then prepare to accept it. Then proceed to improve on the worst."

Burt's advice on Shmoozing works for approaching people and for dealing with life in general. If you can answer Burt's question, "What's the worst that can happen?" you probably can overcome your fears by using the techniques suggested in this book. Keep thinking about Burt's observations and practice the Shmooze techniques and you will ultimately generate terrific results for yourself.

Steve with Brad Pitt (At the Golden Globe Awards).

Brad Pitt

"I believe in sincerity and truth. People will connect with you if you don't bullshit them when you Shmooze them."

Brad Pitt is a terrific person to have as a friend. What you see with him is what you get. We met Brad a number of years ago at the Golden Globe Awards and got a conversation started by talking about his favorite football team, the Pittsburgh Steelers. Over the years, we have become good friends and have been fortunate enough to stay in contact with him and we can vouch for the fact that he lives by his no-nonsense quote above.

Brad Pitt is very straightforward and honest. To Brad, his honesty is his version of Shmoozing because it truly is effective. People do "connect" with him when they come in contact with him and sense his sincerity and straight forwardness. Follow his advice and you too will connect positively with everyone you want to talk to, influence, or Shmooze.

Bret enjoying a friendly golf Shmooze with Joe Pesci (At a Palm Springs Golf Tournament).

Joe Pesci

"There is no Shmoozing situation that a good cigar can't fix!"

Joe Pesci is obviously a big cigar fan. This recommendation of Joe's should remind you of the advice we gave in previous chapters about the wisdom of giving away cigars to get a good Shmooze going.

Using the tried and true good old give-away technique and shrewdly handing out cigars (or food) can certainly help your Shmooze cause, particularly with cigar aficionados and Shmoozers like Joe Pesci.

Bill Murray with Steve (At the celebrity Golf tournament in Pebble Beach).

Bill Murray

"Always go to the bathroom when you have the chance."

Bill is one of the funniest men alive. Just look at his movies "Stripes" and "Meatballs" if you need proof. He told us that it was his humor that made him a good Shmoozer. It is almost impossible for anyone to have a bad conversation with Bill Murray. He has such an original, off beat Shmooze that it goes beyond the scope of this book. Bill is who we look to for inspiration when we need it!

Steve Martin with Steve (At the opening of Steve Martin's play "Picasso at the Lapin Agile").

Steve Martin

"Decide promptly, but never give your reasons. Your decisions may be right, but your reasons are sure to be wrong."

After Steve Martin told us this bit of wisdom, I asked him what his reasoning was behind this concept.

He got the joke quickly! (We're still not sure what he means here. We'll be asking him for a more in-depth answer in our next book!)

Steve is hilarious on the big screen, but typically very serious in his Shmoozing. His best Shmooze technique is the way he uses his incredible talent in conversations with you. He can't hide it, the talent just oozes forth when he speaks to you and you are Shmoozed, charmed and impressed, all at the same time. We recommend you study his technique next time you see him interviewed because

Shmoozing doesn't get any better than talking to Steve Martin. (He's got another new movie coming out shortly and you can watch him Shmoozing it up on the talk show circuit)

Bret with Samuel L. Jackson (At the Oscar Awards).

Samuel L. Jackson

"Be true to yourself and respect your art. That's the best way to Shmooze."

A Shmooze tip that can be gleaned from Samuel is in the advice he gave us when he recommended: If you are comfortable with yourself, first, then you can be comfortable with others. Respect yourself and your capabilities and when you are Shmoozing, your confidence will shine through.

We think Samuel would agree that it is important for you to be sincere and honest in your Shmooze as you will then feel better about asking questions or leading the conversation. This will help contribute to making your whole outward attitude appear to beam which will make you even more effective in your Shmooze.

Bret with Dennis Hopper (At the Billboard Music Awards).

Dennis Hopper

"The Lord had the wonderful advantage of working alone."

In response to our question on Shmoozing, Dennis treads on a subject most savvy Shmoozers should probably avoid—religion. Religion invokes deep feeling in a lot of people and it is difficult to control where a conversation goes once religion becomes the topic. It is also difficult to know precisely what one means when they use religious examples and metaphors to make their points. Smart Shmoozers know to proceed with caution when dealing with controversial subjects. Keep it light and lively, until you know more about your target.

Bob Hope with Bret (At the Comedy Hall of Fame Awards).

Bob Hope

"If you can't sleep, then get up and do something instead of lying there worrying. It's the worry that gets you, not the lack of sleep."

Bob told us that he felt if you are getting involved in the world of Shmooze, don't worry about what you can't initially accomplish. Simply get out there and put forth as much effort as you can.

Eventually you are going to succeed. Bob Hope knows about success, so we recommend you follow his Shmoozing advice and give it the 100% effort. You've got everything to gain.

Steve with Tom Hanks and hair stylist to the stars Michele Hillion (At the Oscar Awards).

Tom Hanks

"Do your best to be interesting."

Tom told us that he believed the more interesting one was in a conversation, the better their chances were that their Shmooze would be successful.

That's easy for Tom to advocate because he's so damn talented that he effortlessly is interesting, no matter what he says. But us unfortunate average folks need to learn Shmoozing techniques so we can start sounding interesting and becoming interesting in our new social interaction and relationships.

You can follow Tom's sage advice and give off the impression of being interesting by incorporating the techniques in Chapter 2 "Shmooze Basics" into your conversational style.

Bret with Robert Downey Jr. and Stone Temple Pilot lead singer Scott Weiland (At the Billboard Music Awards).

Robert Downey Jr.

"You gotta just go up and give it a try. Don't stress about it—just go and Shmooze the person you are interested in."

Robert told us that you shouldn't think too much. You should use your intuition. We might add that if you also combine Robert Downey's advice with the Shmooze techniques from this book, you will do just fine. So, embrace these concepts on Shmoozing and get out there and start practicing them. You will soon see yourself grow as a Shmoozer and, as Robert says, you won't "stress" out. The more you practice the less you'll stress.

Bret with Danny DeVito (At the Golden Globe Awards).

Danny DeVito

"When fate hands you a lemon try to make lemonade."

A nice quote, although a little overused (Who knows, maybe Danny invented it.) For a second we thought this was another Jerry Seinfeld-type effort to confuse us and screw up the best part of our book!

I don't think Danny wanted to be creatively philosophical the day we talked to him about Shmoozing. But his point is important. The best Shmoozers never let rejection get them down. They just keep trying. They keep testing and perfecting their Shmooze, until it starts working.

Steve with Johnny Depp (At the Golden Globe Awards).

Johnny Depp

"Be unique when Shmoozing—don't try to conform to someone else's standards."

Johnny told us that he believed in the virtues of being your own person. Do what you want to do. Be who you want to be.

This is good advice. And you should incorporate these concepts of uniqueness and originality into *your* Shmoozing repertoire. If you think back on your own group of friends, don't you have the most fun with those who are unique and original? Your new acquaintances will also be attracted by uniqueness. We're not suggesting weirdness to become unique, but some solid original ideas, comments, observations, questions—this should be enough for you to get your point across, which should be that you are original, unique and special.

Bret with Willem Defoe (On the set of Speed II).

Willem Defoe

"I don't know too much about it (Shmoozing). I'm just a normal kid from Wisconsin."

Willem is discreetly using the good old "humble" Shmooze technique on us with his sly answer!

This is how the "humble" approach works: When you are in a position of power or are famous, the humble routine is truly a terrific Shmooze method. People expect you to be a little jaded by your success, so the unexpected humbleness comes across to observers as you being down to earth and just a normal, regular guy. Suddenly, you are beloved by everyone in the room because you have the good common sense to carry yourself in a humble, respectful, low-key way like Willem does. (By the way, don't ask about his name "Willem". You can be sure all the bad Shmoozers have already discussed the subject of his unusual name. You should be original and talk about something he hasn't already heard).

Jim Carrey with Steve, next to Lauren Holly (At the tribute dinner to Steven Spielberg).

Jim Carrey

"Just contort your face."

Jim might have the face contortion industry locked up, but when he answered our question on Shmoozing with this advice, we had difficulty coming up with a message to you, our readers, that would give you insight on Jim's Shmoozing philosophy.

One thing is for sure though, if you want an example of using humor to Shmooze, Jim is among the best. Watching his phenomenal success makes us want to Shmooze our way into becoming a famous comedian, just like he Shmoozed his way to the top. Only problem is, he's got the talent—we're still like most of you readers: works in progress.

Steve with Kirstie Alley (At the Emmy Awards).

Kirstie Alley

"Be fun and be sincere when Shmoozing."

Kirstie is correct in that if you are perceived to be fun during a conversation or encounter, people will want to repeat the experience. Her technique and suggestion to use sincerity is also always a wise tip to follow for the aspiring master Shmoozer.

Tom Arnold

"When Shmoozing don't dwell on mistakes. We all make mistakes—the key is to learn from them."

Tom's words ring true. He feels it is important to understand the mistakes you make, move on, and then use the experience as a learning tool. Tom told us that he believes in learning from his mistakes so he can avoid making them again.

If you're the type of person who doesn't make mistakes, then you're lying! It takes a big heart to admit you make a lot of mistakes and Tom always likes to tell it like it is. So, start Shmoozing, and like Tom says, learn from your mistakes.

Woody Allen

"I'm astounded by people who want to know the universe when it's hard enough to find your way around Chinatown."

When we asked Woody how this comment applied to our question on his views about Shmoozing, he just shook his head and rolled his eyes—just like he does in all his great comedy movies. We quickly realized Woody didn't like our questions on Shmoozing so we moved on to another topic, being the competent Shmoozers we are, and got him back on track talking about something he did care about.

We intend to follow up on our question about Shmoozing with Woody again in a future conversation. Stay tuned.

TELEVISION STARS' TRUE CONFESSIONS ON SHMOOZING

George Wendt
Rip Torn
Brooke Shields
Jerry Seinfeld
Roseanne
Paul Reiser
Conan O'Brien
Dennis Miller
Jenny McCarthy
David Letterman
Jay Leno
Larry King

Kelsey Grammer
David Duchovny
Ellen DeGeneres
Walter Cronkite
Cindy Crawford
Joan Collins
Andrew "Dice" Clay
David Caruso
Valerie Bertinelli
Jennifer Anniston
Tim Allen

George Wendt with Bret (At the Emmy Awards).

George Wendt

"My key to life is never eat anything at one sitting that you can't lift."

This is the complex answer George gave us when we asked him about his views on Shmoozing. George is using his well-known sense of humor here to create a winning conversation with us. We have observed that humor is a strong thread in his Shmoozing techniques, even though he didn't admit this to us. Many celebrities like to use the reliable "humor Shmooze" as part of their Shmooze repertoire. You should learn to master it as well.

Rip Torn with Bret (At the Emmy Awards).

Rip Torn

"Persistence would be the strongest attribute of a good Shmoozer. Know what you want and keep focused on the goal."

When we spoke with Rip about Shmoozing, he felt that identifying your goal and then working towards it was a key to success. We spoke earlier in this book about creating a plan when you enter a party—setting a goal to meet certain people (or all of them). Additionally, we can certainly recommend Rip's advice about being persistent. If your Shmooze isn't working, regroup and try again with a different tact. Don't give up. You can succeed—you just need to keep trying.

Rip used an effective Shmooze technique on us—humility. When we complimented him on his Emmy win for *"The Larry Sanders Show"*, he credited Garry Shandling and the rest of the staff for his success. Humility in the face of accomplishments always plays well, and Rip has mastered these attributes. Rip is a talented actor and always very interesting to Shmooze with.

Bret with Brooke Shields (At the American Comedy Awards).

Brooke Shields

"Choose your friends carefully. Your enemies will choose you."

Brooke told us she believed that people should slow down on mass Shmoozing and be more targeted and selective. In other words, do not try to meet and build relationships with everyone, as this will obviously lead to disappointments. Pick your spots, and then strike.

This is the more patient, calm approach to the Shmooze game. If you are as talented as Brooke is, you should take your time! But if you are like Steve and I (we need all the help from Shmoozing that we can get), you will use the Shmooze all the time.

Steve with Jerry Seinfeld (At the Emmy Awards).

Jerry Seinfeld

"Don't take the bull by the horns, take him by the tail, then you can let go when you want to."

What the hell is Jerry talking about with that answer to our question on what he thinks about Shmoozing?

He told us this summed up his views on the subject of Shmoozing. Hmmmmmm...... well, all we can say is we're still not sure what Jerry's advice is but we'll be asking him again at the next party we see him at. And we'll put his real answer in the next book we write!

Bret with Roseanne (At the Emmy Awards).

Roseanne

"Don't be a total bore. If you have something going on, people will respond."

We couldn't agree with Roseanne more. If you think about people you know who are bores, you certainly don't want yourself to ever be considered one. The Shmooze techniques and suggestions in this book give you "something going on" and we guarantee that people will respond to you if you use this information.

Those of you who unfortunately have nothing going on should read this book twice and develop yourselves. This information can be viewed as therapy for your personality. And you can get your therapy a lot cheaper using this book than talking to a shrink! So, follow Roseanne's advice and follow our advice, and you will be on track to being someone with a lot going on in your life.

Steve and Paul Reiser (At the Emmy Awards).

Paul Reiser

"Don't ever slam the door. You may want to back through it."

Paul's advice to us was that you don't burn bridges, and don't step on the little people on the way up... you just might need them on the way down.

Paul is telling it like it really is in life and we should all listen to this advice. This book has taught you to be sincere and interesting to be with during your Shmooze encounters. Don't "slam the door" on future Shmoozing possibilities by being rude to people during your encounters. There's nothing to gain and a lot to lose when the person you dissed finally finds a way to pay you back.

Bret with Conan O'Brien (At the Emmy Awards).

Conan O'Brien

"The secret to creativity is knowing how to hide your sources."

You may be wondering what this has to do with what Conan thinks about Shmoozing? Well our Shmooze discussion moved to the subject of creativity, and Conan, who is one of the most creative people on the planet, smoothly played down his own skills and talent in this area. This self-deprecating humor is very effective and always a great Shmooze technique. Watch this subtle Shmoozer charm his talk show guests, put himself down, and make everyone laugh with his original, wacky, off beat antics.

Dennis Miller with Bret (At the Emmy Awards).

Dennis Miller

"I would think that humor and intelligence would be the most important attributes for Shmoozing. But, you guys do pretty well and you don't seem all that intelligent!"

In one sentence, Dennis was able to Shmooze on multiple levels. First, he was right on the money that humor and intelligence are very, very important. In fact, intelligence often shines through when you display your knowledge and our suggestion to keep up on current events rings true here. If you keep up on your current events, you will have facts and opinions on most subjects that will arise during small talk—and thus, you will seem intelligent. Second, Dennis Shmoozed us with a compliment "You guys do pretty well...", but at the same time he used humor "...and you don't seem all that intelligent!" Dennis is articulate, intelligent, and very, very funny (for proof, just check out "Dennis Miller Live" on HBO). These qualities combine to make him a master Shmoozer.

Steve with Jenny McCarthy (At a fundraiser sponsored by Marvin Davis).

Jenny McCarthy

"I never plan anything. I Just run up and give it a try."

Jenny finds it easy to start conversations and build relationships. Her quote is in response to our question about how she approaches new people. Her lack of nervousness or fear is admirable. If you follow her advice to "Just give it a try"—your Shmoozing will become easier and easier. Jenny is right. What do you have to lose?

David Letterman with Steve (At the Emmy Awards).

David Letterman

"Sometimes something worth doing is worth overdoing."

We asked Dave about what he really meant by this comment on the subject of Shmoozing and he explained that our overdoing the "Shmooze thing" may have proved him wrong. I guess he was breaking our chops about how much Shmoozing we do and how much we both manage to get away with.

Dave shouldn't criticize us too heavily as he is such a super-Shmoozer he's got his own top-rated talk show. Dave is able to Shmooze as good as anyone, thanks mostly to his use of humor.

But he also has a knack of putting people at ease during a conversation, which makes him an especially good Shmoozer. We have met Dave seven or eight times and he has always been terrific to talk to—whether the conversation is Formula One racing or cigars.

Steve with Jay Leno (At the Emmy Awards).

Jay Leno

"Personally I'm always ready to learn, although I do not always like to be taught."

Jay talks about the fine line that exists during conversation. Do not try and preach, or even teach during a casual Shmoozing conversation.

Jay is another celebrity who is very down to earth, has always had time for us whenever we met him at celebrity events, and best of all, he is a terrific person to Shmooze with. Just watch the talent he exudes when interviewing people on his TV talk show. We can all learn a few new Shmooze techniques from observing him work his endless Shmooze genius on his late night TV guests.

Steve with Larry King (At a Hollywood fundraiser).

Larry King

"Your personality is the most important factor when Shmoozing."

Larry told us that to have a good personality you need to have a spark of charisma. We concur with Larry King's observation and remind you to re-read the earlier chapters of this book which are meant to help you develop that interesting and fun, charisma-filled personality that you need for the successful Shmooze. Once you get a flavor of what it takes to have a Shmoozer's personality, you should be able to quickly develop or perfect these traits on your own.

In this book, we are exposing you to a whole range of options that you may never have realized existed. People are not just born as Shmoozers. You can teach yourself to become one if you follow our advice!

Bret and Steve out golfing with Kelsey Grammer (At the Frank Sinatra Invitational Golfing Tournament in Palm Springs).

Kelsey Grammer

"Don't be fake. Say what you mean, but have fun in the process."

Kelsey has been terrific to us. He went out of his way and helped us get our television deal for our humorous new show, *ALL ACCESS*, and has always had time for us at various Hollywood social events.

Kelsey's advice to us on Shmoozing was to be yourself and to always try to have fun because you only live once. Kelsey is the type of Shmoozer who believes that the hearse does not have luggage racks! We agree! Shmooze, have fun, and then Shmooze some more!

Steve with David Duchovny (At the "Playing God" movie premier).

David Duchovny

"At the very least, try to be mildly interesting."

When we had this conversation about Shmoozing with David, he was a little bored from having hoards of fans telling him the same thing all night. We met him at the Emmy Awards and by the time we approached him it was obvious he was frustrated from the onslaught of people coming up to him, each gushing about how big a fan they are.

We, however, used our own good Shmoozing advice and began speaking with David about a non-showbiz subject—Canada (he spends a good deal of his time there). It was a nice break from the monotony of entertainment subjects he was forced to talk about and he seemed to enjoy the conversation. Remember to always try and discuss some topic that your target finds interesting. When meeting celebrities you can be sure that topic usually will not be show business related. Also, as we've pointed out earlier, do not ever be a gushing fan in your initial approach or conversation, as you will be disappointed if your goal was to make a memorable impression on your target. This behavior just bores the hell out of most celebrities who have seen and heard it all from idiotic, goofy, annoying fans.

Steve with Ellen DeGeneres (At the Golden Globe Awards).

Ellen DeGeneres

"You can't go wrong when you're Shmoozing if you offer food."

Ellen told us this was her favorite Shmooze technique and it certainly is a good approach because it forces an immediate reply from your target which then enables you to follow up with additional Shmoozing conversation. Ellen must believe in the old adage that the key to a person's heart is through their stomach. This is another variation of the give-away technique—which is usually very effective. We recommend you follow Ellen's advice, when possible, and if you don't have food handy to give away, then follow the additional sage advice we have prepared for you throughout this book.

Steve with Walter Cronkite (At the American Television Awards).

Walter Cronkite

"Honesty, integrity and loyalty. You can not ask for more."

Mr. Cronkite felt the key to Shmoozing was a straight-ahead approach. He told us he believed people should not play games, just say what you mean and mean what you say. Wait a minute. Would it really still be Shmoozing if you followed this advice?

We guess it would be okay to Shmooze using this approach, but it would be a low key kind of Shmooze, unlike a lot of the aggressive good stuff we've packed this book with and that we recommend you start using!

Steve with Cindy Crawford (At the Emmy Awards).

Cindy Crawford

"Enjoy what you do and be honest with people."

Cindy told us this was her simple secret to success when communicating with people and Shmoozing. It sounds to us like a pretty solid prescription to follow, especially when added to our proven, masterful ideas demonstrated in this book!

Cindy is terrific to talk to and she is always gracious and down to earth. With supermodel/actress Cindy, you have a terrific example of how far a smile can go. Take a lesson from her and smile during your conversations, you will notice that the other people in the conversation will generally smile along and enjoy the interaction with you even more.

Joan Collins

"'No Comment!' is a splendid expression. I am using it these days again and again."

Joan was not very interested in talking with us. But we'll ask her at the next event we find her at, what brilliant advice she can give our readers on the subject of Shmoozing.

Sometimes people feel above any need for courtesy. When they are at that point in their lives, they actually may believe they do not need to Shmooze.

No matter who you are, we advise you to try not to get into this sort of mindset because Shmoozing, as we define it, is a positive, upbeat activity that helps people. Lighten up Alexis!

Valerie Bertinelli

"If you do what you have always done, you'll get what you've always gotten. Shmoozing is definitely something new for most people."

This is another way to say, "Work towards your goals." Do not fall into a routine or procrastinate about doing the things you know you should be doing. Valerie believes in getting out there and doing whatever it takes to meet your goals. Remember, if you act like everyone else, you'll end up like everyone else. That's why you've got to learn our recommended Shmooze techniques, so you can be different than the rest of the people out there and end up where you want to be.

Andrew "Dice" Clay

"Never get married in the morning, cause you never know who you'll meet that night."

The "Dice Man" told us that he Shmoozes by using his special brand of original and outrageous humor. He must be doing something right because even with his often lewd, wild and insulting comments, he somehow managed to sell-out Madison Square Garden and somehow Shmoozed his way into starring in a new prime-time TV show *Hitz* on UPN. Go figure.

Steve with David Caruso (At the Emmy Awards).

David Caruso

"Be honest with yourself and be honest with others. People can sense honesty when you are Shmoozing."

Sincerity is a valuable trait. Never think that you will fool people at the top when you are being phony with them. Practice your Shmooze techniques, follow David Caruso's advice, and never act pretentiously, or like a phony.

In case you weren't clear on this important point, being a Shmoozer is far from being a phony. Remember, the Shmooze is meant to open the door to an encounter that otherwise would never have happened. If you use your Shmooze in a phony way, it will backfire on you. So be real, be honest and put some time into developing your Shmooze so you can also be intelligent in your conversations.

Tim Allen

"Don't be condescending."

Tim gave us this good piece of advice when we asked him about his personal views on Shmoozing. It is difficult to be an effective Shmoozer when you are, at the same time, looking down on the person you are Shmoozing. Comedians like Don Rickles and Rodney Dangerfield are not role models for the art of successful Shmoozing. People with the attitude of savvy Shmoozer, Tim Allen, are!

Treating people respectfully always pays off.

Steve with Jennifer Anniston (At the Golden Globe Awards).

Jennifer Anniston

"If you approach people with whom you have something in common, that is probably the best way to Shmooze."

Or, as our book's Shmooze techniques show you, create something in common with each of your preferred targets.

Jennifer is right by noting the importance of having something in common with the person you approach. But as we have explained, don't feel restricted by the fact that you don't have much in common with the people you'd like to be talking to. That is the whole point of our book! You can skillfully Shmooze your way into *any* conversation you want to be in. Just pick your point of entry and start Shmoozing away! You have got the necessary skills to do the job if you've gotten to this point in our book!

MUSIC STARS' TRUE CONFESSIONS ON SHMOOZING

Barbra Streisand
Rod Stewart
Bruce Springsteen
Diana Ross
Reba McIntyre
Lyle Lovett
Quincy Jones
Garth Brooks
Pat Boone
Bono
Tony Bennett

Barbra Streisand

"There is only one rule for being a good Shmoozer—learn to listen."

This exact concept has been discussed and described previously in this book. Barbara hit it right on the head with this important recommendation. Remember the essential Shmooze technique of being interested in others' interests. If you concentrate on the topics the persons you are speaking to are interested in, you will have half the battle won. Listen to what others are saying and steer your conversational topics on their course.

Steve with Rod Stewart (At the Grammy Awards).

Rod Stewart

"Doing what you like is freedom. Liking what you do is happiness. If you enjoy Shmoozing and it makes you happy, that's what counts."

Wow, can you imagine how easy it is for Rod to write all those great songs when he has the ability to answer questions with profound ideas that sound like lyrics!

We don't know how he instantly came up with this answer, but he seems to be supportive of the concept of Shmoozing. Take his advice and work towards enjoying your Shmoozing when you do it.

You only get one social life, so do not settle. Use your new Shmooze skills to get what you want and to do what you want. That's why we wrote this book: to teach you all of this important stuff that celebrities and people at the top all know!

Bruce Springsteen with Steve (At the Birthday party for Sting after his concert at the Wiltern Theater in Hollywood).

Bruce Springsteen

"Just don't kiss ass."

When we ask Bruce about his views on the subject of Shmoozing he gave us quite a quote! The Boss's answer speaks for itself. As usual, Bruce tells it like it is and doesn't sugar coat things. Surprisingly, Springsteen's approach is almost identical to Walter Cronkite's preference for straight-shooting! (Although Walter did put his ideas on the subject a bit more eloquently).

Diana Ross with Steve (At the Golden Globe Awards).

Diana Ross

"Take care that the face that looks out from the mirror in the morning is a pleasant face. You may not see it again during the day, but others will."

Diana told us that her success in Shmoozing was being as pleasant to others as she possibly could be. This is simple and solid wise advice. It goes back to what we said about Cindy Crawford's smile. If you have a friendly, pleasant attitude and demeanor it will come through in the way you interact with people and the way others perceive you.

Steve with Reba McIntyre (At the Reba "Listening Party" at the Country Star Restaurant in Universal City).

Reba McIntyre

"I tell people I'm too stupid to know what's impossible. I have ridiculously large dreams and half the times they come true."

Reba told us she felt Shmoozers should not limit themselves. She felt that people should go for what they want. The lesson from Reba is: If you go after it—you just might get it! If you dare to dream about achieving something—you just may make it come true!

Lyle Lovett with Bret (At the Grammy Awards).

Lyle Lovett

When we began our Shmooze we discussed Lyle's past relationship with Julia Roberts. He told us:

"It's true that I did get the girl, but then my grandfather always said, 'Even a blind chicken finds a few grains of corn now and then.'"

Lyle seems genuinely very unimpressed with his celebrity. This humbleness is a terrific Shmooze technique that probably has contributed to his success both musically, and for a while, romantically with his ex, Julia Roberts. Humbleness serves to make people more comfortable in a conversation and disarms even the toughest talkers.

Quincy Jones

"When your work speaks for itself, don't interrupt."

Quincy told us that when Shmoozing, you shouldn't brag or concentrate on your own accomplishments. And we certainly agree. As has been advised here previously, top Shmoozers don't talk too much about themselves. They know how to focus on their targets' preferred subjects of discussion and keep the conversation interesting for the persons they are trying to Shmooze.

Pat Boone

"Accept the things to which fate binds you, and love the people with whom fate brings you together, and do so with all your heart."

Can you believe Pat just came up with this deep answer to our question on what he thinks about the fine art of Shmoozing! Pat gave us this advice on Shmoozing which we thought about, deeply appreciated, and then had to reflect and disobey. Just like Brooke Shields, Pat is not a major fan of Shmoozing. But Steve and I are no Pat Boones and neither are you!

So if you regular folk out there want to take serious action and make things happen in your life sooner rather than later, then we think you shouldn't wait for "fate" but, rather, you better work on your Shmooze!

Pat truly loves meeting new people. His sincerity is a so warm and deep, you cannot help but enjoy his company, even if he's not yet a Shmoozer!

Bret with Garth Brooks (At the American Music Awards).

Garth Brooks

"Know what you want and strive to get it."

Garth told us he believes one's Shmooze should have a purpose, a plan and a goal. Garth uses a Shmooze technique that is very powerful. He gives you his undivided attention during a conversation no matter what is going on around him or who is trying to talk to him. You can feel his concentration on your conversation, and this attention drives home the feeling that he really cares about you. I believe he is one of those special people who truly does care what the person he is listening to has to say. He is an extremely giving individual to those who are lucky enough to meet and speak with him. We've had the privilege to Shmooze with him four or five times so we know this side of Garth pretty well. Garth gives great Shmooze!

Bret with U2 lead singer Bono (At the Grammy Awards).

Bono

"Use your life to make a difference in this world. If Shmoozing helps you make a difference, then do it."

In speaking to Bono, we came away agreeing with his philosophical premise. Most people do want to leave a positive mark on the world however, they are not sure how to do it. We all only get one lifetime and the more good we can do with it, the better off the world will be for having each of us as a part of it.

You can use your Shmooze techniques to put yourself into any position or situation you want. Most likely, you will benefit from being in these new situations. Hopefully, you will use your new skills to help others as well. Make your mark. Reach your goals. And, as Bono suggests, do some good.

Steve with Tony Bennett (At the Grammy Awards).

Tony Bennett

"I think one of the reasons I'm popular again is because I'm wearing a tie. When Shmoozing, you have to be different."

We think Tony is popular again because a new generation has discovered his enormous talent. While we are all impressed with his fashion sense, the above quote is a tell-tale sign of his savvy Shmoozing technique. He is making light of his own success and using humor to do it. He was Shmoozing us and we didn't even know it! Humor is a common key to the successful Shmooze.

SPORTS STARS' TRUE CONFESSIONS ON SHMOOZING

Emmitt Smith
Mike Piazza
Sugar Ray Leonard
Charles Barkley
Hank Aaron

Steve with Emmitt Smith (At the ESPY Awards).

Emmitt Smith

"Education is the key. Then you sound like you know what you are talking about when you Shmooze."

With this answer to our Shmooze question, Emmitt is not just talking a good game. He recently followed his own advice and went back to college to finish his degree. Education is very important—both formal, as in college, and informal as discussed previously in this book, through the use of newspapers and the Internet to keep up on current events. The extra knowledge not only gives you fuel for a conversation, but will help you Shmooze your way into being the information source when others are discussing the news.

Mike Piazza with Bret (At the ESPY Awards).

Mike Piazza

"Pick your spots when approaching someone. Make sure not to be too aggressive."

Mike likes his privacy and told us that the most important thing to consider when approaching someone to Shmooze is to respect their space. It is always a good idea to choose a strategic moment to make your Shmoozing approach. As Mike indicates, you don't get a second chance to make a good first impression! Take the extra minutes to begin your Shmooze when its most likely to succeed given the circumstances.

Sugar Ray Leonard

"We're all given some sort of skill in life. Mine just happens to be beating up on people."

In response to our question on his views on developing one's Shmoozing skills, Sugar Ray gave us this funny answer. We would like to reiterate that this book will give you the skill to Shmooze when you're done beating people up or doing whatever it is that you do! With the skill of Shmoozing under your belt, everything is possible. That's why we are advocating that you go out there and apply these concepts and Shmooze.

Charles Barkley

"I truly mean it when I say I am not a role model. I play basketball. That's it."

We asked Charles about his views on shmoozing and he tried to explain to us that we should not care about his thoughts on Shmoozing or his views on life. He made a point of letting us know that he does not take himself too seriously, and that in itself was a successful Shmooze technique. He probably didn't even know that he was Shmoozing us, but he was! And it was effective because he comes off as one of the few down-to-earth athletes who is not affected by his fame.

Hank Aaron with Bret and Frank Gifford (At the Jim Thorpe Sports Awards).

Hank Aaron

"Don't worry about Shmoozing. Be yourself and be honest, and you'll do just fine."

Hank told us he didn't feel Shmoozing was really necessary. It seems as if he's also from the Walter Cronkite school of "what you see is what you get" type of non-Shmoozing.

Well, we believe that a few Shmoozing techniques thrown into the "being yourself" and "honesty" pot won't hurt either, Hank. Trust us on this. We know what we're talking about, I mean Shmoozing about!

BUSINESS AND GOVERNMENT LEADERS' TRUE CONFESSIONS ON SHMOOZING

Zig Ziglar

Donald Trump

Clarence Thomas

Kenneth Starr

Robert Schuller

Antonin Scalia

Dan Quayle

Mike Ovitz

Sandra Day O'Conner

Newt Gingrich

Gerald Ford

Michael Eisner

Johnnie Cochran

Dale Carnegie

Steve with Donald Trump (At the Grammy Awards).

Donald Trump

"If by Shmooze you mean relationship building, then I would say staying in control is important."

"The Donald" told us that to him Shmoozing was a form of "building and strengthening one's relationships". We thought about this for a while and we realized that this definition was the best we had ever heard when it comes to explaining what Shmoozing really is all about. It was also the nicest way to refer to something some would call "manipulation, deception, getting what you want" and worse! Donald's advice, however, has touched the heart of what good Shmoozing is all about. We have been at several celebrity events with Donald and he has always been approachable and gracious to speak with. His Shmooze was effective and left us with the feeling we could chat him up again in the future and he would be happy to talk to us. So we did chat him up again—at several other events—and he was great to talk to each time. Whenever you get that feeling after speaking with a celebrity, you can be sure you've just spoken to a master Shmoozer. To find out more about how Donald Trump Shmoozes you'll have to check out his new book, *The Art of the Comeback* !

Zig Ziglar

"Winning is not everything, but the effort to win is."

We asked Zig to explain this quote and exactly how it applied to Shmoozing. He told us that if you want to be successful at anything, including Shmoozing, you have got to give it your best effort. He is obviously right. Start practicing your Shmoozing and keep practicing so *you* can give it *your* best effort.

Bret and Steve with Supreme Court Justice Clarence Thomas (At the U.S. Supreme Court dinner).

Supreme Court Justice Clarence Thomas

"This cigar doesn't hurt your Shmoozing cause!"

We gave Justice Thomas a nice cigar when we met (Shmoozed) him at a recent Supreme Court dinner, and he was very appreciative. When we asked him about whether he used any Shmoozing techniques, he laughed and told us that the cigar give-away was a nice touch in our Shmoozing act. He said he doesn't use any Shmoozing tricks, he just acts as his regular self and has no problem communicating.

Some people are naturals at the fine art of conversation and don't think they need to consciously work on their Shmooze. We, however, do not believe in being unprepared, and we feel that a good Shmooze is like preparing for your final exams: the more you study the better you'll do! As a side note, there is no need to try this cigar Shmooze in the future with Justice Thomas, as he told us he is giving them up.

Bret and Steve with Whitewater Independent Counsel Kenneth Starr (At the U.S. Supreme Court dinner).

Kenneth Starr

"Don't be phony—be straightforward in your conversations with people. And avoid being trite, have something meaningful to say."

As the Independent Counsel in the Whitewater affair, and the predicted next Republican Supreme Court nominee, Mr. Starr prefers serious, meaningful conversations when interacting with someone.

This advice on Shmoozing is very solid as Starr has made several important observations about communication. He has identified four really key points we should all remember: Don't be a phony, be straightforward, don't be trite, and have something to say. Unfortunately, when we spoke to him, we violated a few of his key points by discussing many trite issues (common acquaintances, various law schools), but he seemed to enjoy himself while Shmoozing with us, nevertheless.

Robert Schuller

"I'd rather attempt to do something great and fail than to attempt to do nothing and succeed."

Again the theme is similar to Zig Ziglar's advice. Robert told us that you have to always remember to make the effort to first try something in order for you to succeed. He believes people should take a few risks. Do not be afraid to try new things and new social skills, such as Shmoozing.

Bret and Steve with Justice Scalia and former FBI director William Sessions (At the U.S. Supreme Court Dinner).

Supreme Court Justice Antonin Scalia

"I find asking about hometowns is a good icebreaker for me."

In talking to Justice Scalia on the subject of Shmoozing and communication techniques, we were amused to find out that even one of the greatest legal minds in the World also finds it necessary and appropriate to use the Shmooze. The Supreme Court Justices host a number of get-togethers every year and meet hundreds of people. Justice Scalia has even developed his own Shmoozing tips, as revealed in his quote above. You can modify our advice and Justice Scalia's advice with your own unique approach to starting and maintaining a good Shmooze.

Dan Quayle with Bret (At Dan's Book Signing in Crown Books, Torrance, CA).

Dan Quayle

"Qualities like hard work and loyalty are indispensable."

When we asked former Vice President Dan Quayle about his views on the subject of Shmoozing, he answered by referring to tangible qualities to describe the best way to endear yourself to someone.

There is a lot to be said about both hard work and loyalty. If you can successfully generate the perception, among those you are speaking to, that you possess these qualities, you will be way ahead of the game when you are out there Shmoozing someone.

Mike Ovitz

"Be careful what you swallow."

Mike's response to our question on Shmoozing refers to the old adage, "Be careful what you wish for, because you might just get it." For instance, If you try to Shmooze an entire room full of people at a party, are you prepared for what would happen if you were very successful and had 40 new people calling you at home, wanting to be your friend?

Mike Ovitz is saying that you should be careful about what you go after. He also told us that he believes in hard work to get what you're after—very hard work. But at the same time, there is not a better Shmoozer alive. Mike can make you feel so comfortable with him and so safe under his guidance that success in the entertainment field is assured. His methods of motivation, salesmanship and Shmoozing are legendary and make him one of the true masters in the fine art of the Shmooze.

Bret and Steve with Supreme Court Justice Sandra Day O'Connor (At the U.S. Supreme Court dinner).

Sandra Day O'Connor

"There is no substitute for hard work."

Justice O'Connor, one of the top jurists in the country, obtained her position through her legal talents and her incredible dedication to the law. However, we're still not too sure what her position is on the subject of Shmoozing. She sidestepped the question, as a few others have also done, and gave us a generic answer that you rally can't argue with. We'll ask her again the next time we Shmooze her!

Steve with Newt Gingrich (Outside the U.S. Congress).

Newt Gingrich

"We're all human and we all goof. Do things that may occasionally be wrong, but do something."

When we asked Newt for his advice on success in today's world and whether he advocated Shmoozing, he told us that he felt people need to be action orientated. His focus was that people need to be doers. Waiting around for others to do something for you is a waste of time. He advocates taking charge of your lives.

Wise advice from a political Shmoozer who is among the best. You don't Shmooze your way into being the Speaker of the House of Representatives without having a very serious and persuasive Shmooze rap!

Steve with President Ford (At the fundraiser sponsored by Marvin Davis).

President Gerald R. Ford

"When people approach me I like to hear their thoughts on how to improve our country."

Always the patriot, President Ford is still interested in doing what he can to help the country. And this is exactly how he likes to be Shmoozed by people that approach him. It all goes back to being interested in what your target is interested in.

So, if you attempt to Shmooze President Ford, tell him how you think the country could be improved—he's interested in that sort of stuff. Then you can steer the conversation to the real things that are on your mind.

Bret with Michael Eisner (At the fundraiser sponsored by Marvin Davis).

Michael Eisner

"I think you guys are doing fine. You don't need any help from me."

Obviously this is a man who is keenly aware of the skills required to master the art of the Shmooze. We took his comments to us as a compliment. At least we think they were meant as a compliment?

Our Shmooze with Michael Eisner proved to be successful because after we talked he personally got us a meeting over at Disney Television so that we could pitch our idea for a television series. That meeting really got the ball rolling. We ended up signing a deal with the company that produces "America's Funniest Home Videos" and our new TV show *All Access* is soon to be released! Thanks for your help Mr. Eisner!

Bret with Johnny Cochran and lead singer of Baby Spice, Brittney Saxon (At the Loyola Law School party).

Johnny Cochran

"Work hard and position yourself so you are ready for anything. That's the best advice for Shmoozing!"

As lawyer to the stars, Johnny Cochran has stated that the accomplished Shmoozer needs to be on his/her toes and ready for any situation.

With practice, the Shmooze techniques described in this book will help you out of any verbal jam. You will be able to get through even the hardest conversations like a pro. Your preparation should position yourself to enjoy and maximize your new-found skills.

Dale Carnegie

"Most of the important things in the world have been accomplished by people who have kept on trying when there seemed to be no help at all."

Many of the quotes we received for this section of our book have a common theme of "working hard" and "doing it yourself" because others will not always be there to help you. When we asked Dale about his views on Shmoozing he went down the familiar road of advocating hard work and determination. We do concur that if you want to succeed in Shmoozing, it does take hard work. This advice is of course very valuable and very obvious. We agree with Dale and believe that Shmoozing is one of the things that will help you to help yourself if you just keep trying.

George Bush

"Hard work always pays off."

When we met President Bush at a fundraising event for the Republican party, in Washington, D.C., we asked him about his feelings on Shmoozing. He gave us a shrewd and intelligent answer that no one could argue with, that is, no one except us. We believe in hard work, but we also believe in winning results and that's why we advocate Shmoozing. Shmoozing tilts the odds in *your* favor! And Shmoozing is also hard work when it's done right. It is tough to be a politician and not be a great Shmoozer. You have to meet hundreds of people a week and make each one feel special enough to vote for you. Politicians are born Shmoozers. They wouldn't get elected if they weren't. And if you make it to the presidency it means your so good that you've out-Shmoozed them all.

11

CONCLUSION

Congratulations! With the knowledge you now possess, you are well on your way to being a Master Shmoozer!

The only thing left to do is practice. Get out there and Shmooze. The techniques you have learned in this book work, and work well. Remember to use all of the new concepts we've identified and incorporate them into your conversational methods. You will develop the confidence to talk with anyone, anytime, anywhere. And, most importantly, you will get what you want.

Stay focused and relaxed. Have fun along the way. You now have the tools to become a Master Shmoozer, so get out there and get the experience.

We would love to hear about your future Shmooze successes, so please drop us a note about any especially interesting experiences you've had as a result of Shmoozing:

Bret Saxon c/o
SPI BOOKS
136 W. 22nd Street
Fourth Floor
New York, NY 10011

We hope you've enjoyed this book and that you put these techniques to use to better your personal and business relationships and your life.

Your newfound Shmooze skills are powerful. Please remember to use them for good, not evil.

APPENDIX A:

MIXED DRINK RECIPES

The expert Shmoozer has to become an expert mixologist. Luckily for you, this section is your cheat sheet. Whether you are planning a quiet evening for two or a dinner party for 50, the key to a successful Shmooze is pleasing your guests. Your guests will most likely be interested in some sort of alcoholic drinks. So, be prepared!

We will start out by making sure you have the right tools for you to create a wide range of cocktails. The last impression you want to convey to your guests is that you are an unsophisticated, ill-prepared, bad host with minimal social graces and that you can't afford to stock your home bar with basic amounts of popular alcohol. To avoid this sort of an appearance, the following is a list of tools and accessories, which will create a well-stocked bar:

> A jigger measure ¼ oz. to 1½ oz.
> A long bar spoon
> Can & bottle opener
> Bar strainer
> Cocktail shaker
> Ice bucket and tongs
> Pitcher
> Electric blender
> Cocktail glasses
> Goblets
> High ball glasses
> Shot glasses
> Brandy glasses

Once you have collected the proper basic tools, you must stock your bar. You should stock your bar with a variety of Spirits, Mixers, Juices, Soft Drinks, Waters, Creams and Garnishes.

Here is an easy guide to follow to make sure you have the basics. We have also taken the liberty of recommending appropriate quantities of alcohol for your next party:

	10-20 guests	21-40 guests
Vodka	2-3 liters	4 liters
Rum	1-2 liters	2 liters
Brandy	1 liter	1 liter
Beer	1-2 cases	3 cases
Wine	1 case	2 cases
Whiskey	1 liter	2 liters

Bourbon	1 liter	1 liter
Tequila	1-2 liters	2 liters
Dry Vermouth	½ liter	1 liter
Scotch	1-2 liters	3 liters
Gin	1-2 liters	3 liters

After your bar is stocked with a well-rounded variety, you are ready to start serving. The following is a list of the most popular drinks recipes to ensure a very unforgettable evening. (You might want to discreetly hide this book near your bar so you can consult it when someone asks for a difficult drink that you've forgotten how to make).

BOURBON DRINKS

Bourbon Collins

1 ¼ oz. Bourbon
½ oz. Lime juice
½ tsp. Bar sugar
sparkling water

Mix all ingredients except water in a shaker. Shake well and pour into chilled glass over ice and fill with water. Garnish with a lime twist.

Bourbon Sidecar

¾ oz. Bourbon
½ oz. Triple sec
½ oz. Lemon juice

Mix all ingredients with crushed ice in a shaker. Shake well and pour into chilled glass.

Bourbon Sloe Gin Fizz

¾ oz. Bourbon
½ oz. Sloe Gin
1 tsp. Lemon juice
1 tsp. Simple Syrup
sparkling water

Mix all ingredients except water into a chilled glass over ice cracked ice and fill with water. Garnish with a strawberry.

Frozen Mint Julep

1 ¼ oz. Bourbon
1 oz. Lime juice
1 oz. Simple Syrup
6 Fresh Mint Leaves

Combine all ingredients in a glass. Pour into a blender with ½ cup cracked ice and blend at low speed until slushy. Pour into chilled glass and garnish with a mint sprig.

Sweet and Sour Bourbon

1 ¼ oz. Bourbon
3 oz. Orange juice
1 oz. lemon juice
¼ tsp. Bar sugar
1 dash salt

Mix all ingredients with cracked ice in a shaker. Shake well and strain into chilled glass. Garnish with a cherry.

BRANDY & COGNAC DRINKS

Alexander's Sister

¾ oz. Cognac
½ oz. Crème de menthe
1 oz. Heavy cream

Shake well with ice, strain into a chilled glass.

Almond Frost

½ oz. Cognac
¾ oz. Amaretto
1 oz. Orange Juice
½ oz. Cream of coconut
1 oz. Heavy cream
8 oz. Crushed ice

Mix ingredients in blender till smooth and pour into a chilled glass.

Applecar

¾ oz. Cognac
½ oz. Triple sec
1 oz. lemon Juice

Shake ingredients with ice and strain into a chilled glass.

Apricot Cocktail

1 oz. Apricot brandy
¼ oz. gin
2/3 oz. Orange Juice
2/3 oz. Lemon juice

Shake ingredients with ice and strain into a chilled glass.

Apricot Fizz

1 ¼ oz. Apricot brandy
juice of a ½ lime
½ tsp. Bar sugar
4 oz. Club soda

Shake Brandy lime & sugar with ice. Strain into a highball glass over ice and club soda.

Betsy Ross Cocktail

¾ oz. Cognac
½ oz. Port
1 dash triple sec
1 dash bitters

Stir ingredients with ice and strain into a chilled glass.

Bossa Nova

¾ oz. Apricot brandy
¼ oz. Dark rum
1/4 oz. Godiva liqueur
4 oz. Pineapple Juice
¼ oz. Lime juice

Stir ingredients well with crushed ice and strain into a chilled glass.

Brandy Sour

1 ¼ oz. brandy
Juice of ½ lemon
½ tsp. Bar sugar
Shake ingredients with ice
and strain into a chilled
glass. Garnish with lemon
slice and cherry.

Foreign Affair

¾ oz. Cognac
½ oz. Anisette
Stir with ice and strain into
a chilled glass.

Hearts

1 ¼ oz. Cherry brandy
5 oz. Lemon-lime soda
Combine in an ice-cube
filled glass and garnish with
a cherry.

Jelly Bean

½ oz. Blackberry
brandy
½ oz. whiskey
¼ oz. Anisette
Shake well with crushed ice
and strain into a chilled
glass.

Muddy River

1 ¼ oz. Coffee brandy
3 oz. Half & Half
4 oz. Crushed ice
Shake ingredients and pour
into glass.

Root Beer

1 oz. Coffee brandy
¼ oz. Vodka
¼ oz. Galliano
4 oz. Cola
Pour liqueurs into ice filled
beer mug. Fill with cola

Stinger

¾ oz. brandy
½ oz. Crème de cocoa
Mix ingredients and pour
on the rocks.

Sunset

1 ¼ oz. Cherry brandy
4 oz. Orange Juice
Shake well and serve on the
rocks.

CORDIALS & LIQUEUR DRINKS

Amaretto Sour

1 ¼ oz. Amaretto
4 oz. Sweet and sour
4 oz. Crushed ice
Shake ingredients and serve
into a glass.

Amaretto Spritzer

1 ¼ oz. Amaretto
4 oz. Club soda
Pour over ice and stir
gently.

Blue Lagoon

1 ¼ oz. Blue curacao
5 oz. Lemon-lime soda
Combine in an ice-filled
highball glass and garnish
with lemon slice.

Blue Monday

¼ oz. Blue curacao
1 oz. Vodka
Stir well with crushed ice
and strain into chilled
cocktail glass. Garnish with
lemon twist.

Burnt Almond

1 ¼ oz. Amaretto
2 oz. Half & Half
Shake well and serve over
crushed ice.

Cranberry Cooler

1 ¼ oz. Amaretto
2 oz. Cranberry juice
4 oz. Orange juice
Pour Amaretto and
Cranberry juice in an ice
filled chilled glass. Fill with
orange juice.

Fuzzy Navel

1 ¼ oz. Peach schnapps
6 oz. Orange juice
Combine in an ice-filled
highball glass.

Grasshopper

¾ oz. Green crème de
menthe
½ oz. White crème de
cocoa
4 oz. Half & Half
Mix in blender until
smooth and serve in a
chilled glass.

Lovebird

1 ¼ oz. Amaretto
1 oz. Half & Half
Blend in a blender with a
scoop of crushed ice.

Muscle Beach

¾ oz. Triple sec
½ oz. Vodka
8 oz. Pink lemonade
Combine in an ice-filled
highball glass and garnish
with lemon slice.

New Wave

1 ¼ oz. Peach Schnapps
4 oz. Orange juice
1 splash soda
Combine in an ice-filled
highball glass and garnish
with lemon slice.

Pink Squirrel

1 oz. Crème de noya
1 tbsp. White crème de
cocoa
1 tbsp. Light cream
Shake with ice and strain
into chilled glass.

Peppermint Treat

1 oz. Peppermint
schnapps
¾ oz. Green crème de
menthe
1 oz. Heavy cream
Shake well with crushed ice
and strain into chilled glass.
Garnish with cherry.

Rainbow

½ oz. Grenadine
1 oz. Vodka
5 oz. Collins mix
½ oz. Blue curaco
Pour grenadine in
margarita glass. Fill with
crushed ice. Combine
Vodka and Collins Mix in
shaker and pour into glass.
Top with Blue Curaco.

Razzaretto

¾ oz. Raspberry
Schnapps
½ oz. Amaretto
3 oz. Club soda
Pour over ice cube filled
glass.

Sex on the Beach

½ oz. melon liqueur
½ oz. Raspberry liqueur
¼ oz. Vodka
4 oz. Pineapple juice
6 oz. Crushed ice
Shake well with crushed ice
and pour into highball
glass.

Sidecar

¾ oz. Triple sec
½ oz. Cognac
¾ oz. Lemon juice
Shake well with crushed ice
and strain into chilled glass.
Garnish with a twist of
lemon peel.

Sloe Gin Fizz

1 ¼ oz. Sloe Gin
½ tsp. Bar sugar
1 oz. Lemon juice
6 oz. Club soda
Shake Sloe Gin, sugar and
lemon juice and strain into
chilled glass with ice. Top
with soda and stir.

Sweetheart Sip

1 ¼ oz. Amaretto
2 oz. Pineapple juice
Shake well with crushed ice
and strain into chilled glass.
Garnish with orange slice.

Toasted Almond

¾ oz. Coffee liqueur
½ oz. Amaretto
1 oz. Heavy cream
Shake in tumbler and pour
over ice.

Witches Tail

1 oz. Wild berry schnapps
¼ oz. Blue Curaco
3 oz. Sweet and sour

3 oz. Club soda
Combine in an ice-filled
collins glass and garnish
with orange.

GIN DRINKS

Alexander

¾ oz. Gin
½ oz. Crème de Cocoa
1 oz. Heavy cream
Combine all ingredients
with crushed ice in a shaker
and strain into chilled glass.
Garnish with nutmeg.

Barnum

¾ oz. Gin
½ oz. Apricot Brandy
2 dashed bitters
Shake well with crushed ice
and strain into chilled glass.

Belmont

1 ¼ oz. Gin
¾ oz. Half & Half
½ oz. Raspberry syrup
Stir with crushed ice and
strain into chilled glass.

Blue Devil

1 oz. Gin
¼ oz. Blue Curaco
1//2. Lemon juice
Shake well with crushed ice
and strain into chilled glass.
Garnish with lemon slice.

Blue Moon Cock-tail

¾ oz. Gin
½ oz. Blue Curaco
Shake well with crushed ice
and strain into chilled glass.
Garnish with lemon peel.

Boomerang

1 oz. Gin
¼ oz. Dry vermouth
½ oz. Lime juice
Shake well with crushed ice
and strain into chilled glass.
Garnish with lime slice.

Colonial Cocktail

1 ¼ oz. Gin
1 tsp. Maraschino liqueur
½ oz. Grapefruit juice
Combine all with cracked
ice in a shaker. Shake well
and strain into chilled glass.

Colony Club

1 oz. Gin
1 tsp. Pernod
4 dashed orange bitters
Combine all with cracked
ice in a shaker. Shake well
and strain into chilled glass.

Copperstown Cocktail

1 oz. Gin
1/8 oz. Dry Vermouth
1/8 oz. Sweet Vermouth
Combine all with cracked
ice in a shaker. Shake well
and strain into chilled glass.
Garnish with mint sprig.

Derby

1 oz. Gin
¼ oz. Peach brandy
Shake with ice and strain
over crushed ice in a wine
glass.

Dry Martini

1 oz. Gin
1/8 oz. Dry Vermouth
Stir with ice and strain into
a chilled glass. Garnish with
an olive.

Fifty-Fifty

½ oz. Gin
½ oz. Dry Vermouth
Stir with ice and strain into
a chilled glass. Garnish with
an olive.

Fino Martini

1 ¼ oz. Gin
1 tsp. Fino sherry
Stir with ice and strain into
a chilled glass. Garnish with
a lemon twist.

French Rose

½ oz. Gin
½ oz. Cherry Brandy
½ oz. Cherry Liqueur
Shake with crushed ice and
strain into a chilled glass.

Gibson Martini

1 oz. Gin
¼ oz. Dry Vermouth
Stir with ice and strain into
a chilled glass. Garnish with
a twist of lemon peel and
serve with 3 pearl onions.

Gimlet

1 ¼ oz. Gin
¼ oz. Lime juice
Shake with ice and strain
into a chilled glass.

Gin and Ginger

1 ¼ oz. Gin
Ginger Ale
Pour Gin into a chilled
highball glass. Twist lemon
over glass and fill with
ginger ale. Stir gently.

Gin and Tonic

1 ¼ oz. Gin
6 oz. Tonic water
Pour gin over ice in a
highball glass. Fill with
tonic water.

Gin Margarita

1 oz. Gin
¼ oz. Triple sec
Juice of ½ lime
Shake with ice and serve in
a margarita glass rimmed
with salt.

Gin Cooler

1 ¼ oz. Gin
½ tsp. Bar sugar
Sparkling Water
Mix Gin with sugar in a
collins glass. Add ice cubes
and fill with water. Garnish
with lemon peel.

Gin Rickey

1 ¼ oz. Gin
Juice of ½ lime
6 oz. Club soda
Mix Gin with juice in a
highball glass. Add ice
cubes and fill with soda.
Garnish with lime wedge.

Gin Sidecar

¾ oz. Gin
½ oz. Triple sec
1 oz. Lemon juice
Mix ingredients with
cracked ice in a shaker.
Pour into a chilled glass.

Gin Sling

1 ¼ oz. Gin
1 tsp. Bar sugar
1 tsp. Water
juice of ½ lemon
Dissolve sugar and lemon
juice in water. Add ice and
gin. Garnish with lemon
peel.

Gin Sour

1 ¼ oz. Gin
Juice ½ lemon
½ tsp. Bar sugar
Shake with ice and strain into a chilled glass. Garnish with lemon slice and cherry.

Golden Daze

¾ oz. Gin
½ oz. Peach brandy
1 oz. Orange juice
Mix with cracked ice. Shake well and strain into a chilled collins glass.

Golf Cocktail

1 oz. Gin
¼ oz. Dry vermouth
3 dashed bitters
Mix with cracked ice. Shake well and strain into a chilled collins glass.

Grapefruit Cocktail

1 ¼ oz. Gin
¾ oz. Grapefruit Juice
Mix with cracked ice. Shake well and strain into a chilled collins glass.

Hawaiian Cocktail

1 oz. Gin
¼ oz. Triple sec
½ oz. Pineapple Juice
Mix with cracked ice. Shake well and strain into a chilled collins glass.

Homestead Cocktail

¾ oz. Gin
½ oz. Sweet vermouth
Mix with cracked ice. Shake well and strain into a chilled collins glass.
Garnish with orange slice.

Hula-Hula

1 ¼ oz. Gin
1 oz. Orange Juice
1 tbsp. Triple sec
Mix with cracked ice. Shake well and strain into a chilled collins glass.

Kir Gin Cocktail

1 oz. Gin
¼ oz. Crème de cassis
4 oz. Club soda
Pour gin and cassis over ice in a wineglass and fill with club soda. Stir and garnish with a lemon twist.

Knickerbocker

1 oz. Gin
1/8 oz. Dry vermouth
1/8 oz. Sweet vermouth
Mix with cracked ice. Shake well and strain into a chilled collins glass.
Garnish with lemon peel.

Long Island Ice Tea

¼ 1 oz. Gin
¼ oz. Vodka
¼ oz. White rum
¼ oz. Tequila
¼ oz. Triple sec
1 oz. sweet and sour
6 oz. Cola
Fill collins glass with ice add all ingredients except cola. Stir. Add cola to fill. Garnish with lemon wedge.

Martini

¾ oz. Gin
½ oz. Dry vermouth
Stir with ice. Strain into a chilled cocktail glass.
Garnish with an olive.

Melon Cocktail

1 oz. Gin
¼ oz. Maraschino liqueur
½ oz. Lime juice
Mix with cracked ice. Shake well and strain into a chilled cocktail glass.
Garnish with cherry and lemon twist.

Mississippi Mule

1 oz. Gin
¼ oz. Crème de cassis
½ oz. Lemon juice
Mix with cracked ice. Shake well and strain into a chilled collins glass.

Montmartre

1 oz. Gin
¼ oz. Sweet vermouth
¼ oz. White curaco
Mix with cracked ice. Shake well and strain into a chilled cocktail glass.

Moonshot

1 ¼ oz. Gin
3 oz. Clam juice
1 dash Tabasco sauce
Mix with ice cubes. Mix well and pour into a glass.

Newberry

¾ oz. Gin
½ oz. Sweet vermouth
½ tsp. Triple sec
Mix with cracked ice. Shake well and strain into a chilled collins glass.
Garnish with a lemon twist.

Opera

¾ oz. Gin

¼ oz. Littet Rouge
1/8 oz. Maraschino
liqueur
Mix with cracked ice. Shake
well and strain into a
chilled collins glass.

Orange Blossom

1 ¼ oz. Gin
1 oz. Orange juice
Shake with ice. Shake well
and strain into a chilled
cocktail glass rimmed with
sugar. Garnish with orange
slice.

Paisley Martini

1 oz. Gin
½ tsp. Dry vermouth
½ tsp. Scotch
Mix with cracked ice. Shake
well and strain into a
chilled cocktail glass.

Park Avenue

1 oz. Gin
¼ oz. Sweet vermouth
½ oz. Pineapple juice
Mix with cracked ice. Shake
well and strain into a
chilled cocktail glass.

Parisian

½ oz. Gin
½ oz. Dry vermouth
¼ oz. Crème de cassis
Shake with ice. Strain into a
chilled cocktail glass.

Pink Pussycat

1 ¼ oz. Gin
Pineapple Juice
1 dash Grenadine
Pour gin in a chilled
highball glass over ice. Fill
with juice and Grenadine.

Stir gently and garnish with
pineapple spear.

Racquet Club Cocktail

1 oz. Gin
¼ oz. Dry vermouth
1 dash orange bitters
Mix with cracked ice. Shake
well and strain into a
chilled cocktail glass.

Resolute Cocktail

¾ oz. Gin
½ oz. Apricot Brandy
½ oz. Lemon juice
Mix with cracked ice. Shake
well and strain into a
chilled cocktail glass.

Saketini

1 oz. Gin
¼ oz. Sake
Mix with cracked ice. Shake
well and strain into a
chilled cocktail glass.
Garnish with a lemon twist.

Gin Gimlet

1 ¼ oz. Dry Gin
¾ oz. Lime juice
Fill a cocktail glass with ice.
Add gin and lime juice. Stir.
Garnish with slice of lime.

Gin Lemonade

1 ¼ oz. Dry Gin
6 oz. Lemonade
Pour gin over ice in a
highball glass. Add
lemonade. Stir. Garnish
with slice of lemon.

Gin Salty Dog

1 ¼ oz. Dry Gin
6 oz. Grapefruit juice
Pour gin over ice in a tall

glass rimmed with salt. Fill
with juice and stir.

Pink Lemonade

1 ¼ oz. Dry Gin
6 oz. Pink Lemonade
Pour gin over ice in a
highball glass and add
lemonade. Garnish with
slice of lemon.

Sunburn

1 ¼ oz. Dry Gin
5 oz. Lemon-lime soda
Cranberry juice
Fill a highball glass with ice.
Add gin and soda. Fill with
juice. Garnish with slice of
orange.

Silver Shell

¾ oz. Gin
½ oz. Jagermeister
1/8 oz. lemon juice
Mix with cracked ice. Shake
well and strain into a
chilled cocktail glass.
Garnish with a lemon twist.

Snowball

¾ oz. Gin
½ oz. Pernod
½ oz. Half & Half
Mix with cracked ice. Shake
well and strain into a
chilled cocktail glass.
Garnish with a lemon twist.

Sweet Martini

¾ oz. Gin
½ oz. Sweet Vermouth
Stir with ice. Strain into a
chilled cocktail glass.
Garnish with an olive.

Tom Collins

1 ¼ oz. Gin
1 tsp. Bar sugar

Juice of ½ lemon
6 oz. Club soda
Shake gin, lemon and sugar. Strain over crushed ice into a tall glass. Fill with soda. Stir. Garnish with a lemon slice.

White Alexander

¾ oz. Gin
½ oz. Crème de cocoa
1 oz. Half & Half
Shake with ice and strain into a chilled cocktail glass.

RUM DRINKS

Anna's Wish

¾ oz. Dark rum
½ oz. Triple sec
6 oz. Pineapple juice
Pour all ingredients over ice. Stir.

Bat Bite

1 ¼ oz. Dark rum
4 oz. cranberry juice
Pour all ingredients over ice in a highball glass. Stir. Drop a lime wedge into drink.

Black Devil

1 oz. Dark rum
¼ oz. Dry Vermouth
Shake ingredients with ice and strain into chilled cocktail glass. Garnish with black olive.

Black Widow

¾ oz. Dark rum
½ oz. Southern Comfort
1 oz. Sweet and Sour
Shake with ice and strain

into cocktail glass. Garnish with lemon twist.

Bolero Cocktail

1 oz. Dark rum
¼ oz. Apple Brandy
2 dashes Sweet Vermouth
Stir ingredients with ice and strain into chilled cocktail glass.

Breeze Punch

1 ¼ oz. Dark rum
3 oz. Fruit juice
1 oz. Sweet & Sour
Shake ingredients with ice and strain into chilled cocktail glass.

Brown Derby

1 ¼ oz. Dark rum
½ oz. Lime Juice
1/6 oz. Maple Syrup
Shake well with ice and strain over ice cubes into chilled cocktail glass. Garnish with lime wedge.

Cuba Libre

1 ¼ oz. Dark rum
Juice of ½ lime
6 oz. cola
Fill collins glass with ice cubes. Add rum and juice. Top with cola. Garnish with lime slice.

Daquiri

1 ¼ oz. Dark rum
Juice of ½ lime
1 tsp. Bar sugar
Shake ingredients with ice and strain into chilled cocktail glass.

Havana Beach Cocktail

1 ¼ oz. Dark rum
1 ¼ oz. Pineapple juice
4 dashed lemon juice
Shake ingredients with ice and strain into chilled cocktail glass.

Hurricane

¾ oz. Dark rum
½ oz. Rum
Juice of ½ lime
1 tbsp. Fruit juice
Mix rums and juice. Shake well. Pour into an ice-filled glass. Garnish with lime wedge.

Lounge Lizard

1 ¼ oz. Dark rum
3 oz. Orange Juice
1 ½ oz. Cranberry Juice
Pour ingredients over. Serve in a chilled cocktail glass.

Mai Tai

1 oz. Dark rum
¼ oz. Curaco
1 tsp. Grenadine
juice of ½ lime
1 tsp. Bar sugar
Shake ingredients with ice and strain over ice cubes into glass. Garnish with lime slice.

Mary Pickford

1 ¼ oz. Dark rum
1 ¼ oz. Pineapple Juice
3 dashes Grenadine
Shake ingredients with ice and strain into chilled cocktail glass.

Sharkbite

1 ¼ oz. Dark rum
3 oz. Orange Juice
1 dash Grenadine
Pour over ice in a chilled glass.

Palm Beacher

1 oz. Dark rum
¼ oz. Amaretto
6 oz. Orange Juice
Pour over ice in a chilled glass. Stir.

Pina Colada

1 ¼ oz. Dark rum
2 oz. Pineapple Juice
1 oz. Cream of coconut
4 oz. crushed ice
Blend until smooth. Pour into wineglass. Garnish with pineapple stick.

R&B

1 ¼ oz. Spiced rum
2 oz. Orange Juice
2 oz. Pineapple juice
1 splash Grenadine
Pour over ice in a chilled glass.

Rum & Cola

1 ¼ oz. Dark rum
6 oz. Cola
Pour over ice in a chilled glass.

Rum & Ginger

1 ¼ oz. Dark rum
6 oz. Ginger Ale
Pour over ice in a chilled glass.

Rum Julep

1 ¼ oz. Dark rum
1/6 oz. Simple syrup
2 mint leaves
In a glass, muddle syrup with mint, fill glass with ice and pour in rum, stir.

Rum Rickey

1 ¼ oz. Dark rum
Juice of ½ lime
6 oz. Club Soda
Pour rum & lime over ice in a chilled glass, add soda. Stir. Garnish with lime wedge.

Rum Sour

1 ¼ oz. Dark rum
Juice of ½ lemon
½ tsp. Bar sugar
Shake with ice. Strain into chilled highball glass. Garnish with lemon and cherry.

Rummy Sour

1 ¼ oz. Spiced rum
1 ¾ oz. lemon-lime soda
8 oz. crushed ice
Blend in blender with crushed ice until smooth.

Sunny Sour

1 ¼ oz. Dark rum
¼ oz. lemon juice
½ tsp. Bar sugar
Shake rum, lemon & sugar with crushed ice. Strain into cocktail glass. Garnish with lemon wedge.

Waikiki Tiki

1 ¼ oz. Dark rum
3 oz. Orange juice
2 oz. Pineapple juice
Pour over ice in a glass and stir.

Wrath of Grapes

1 ¼ oz. Dark rum
4 oz. Grape juice
1 oz. sweet & Sour
Mix in an ice-filled collins glass and stir. Garnish with pineapple spear.

SCOTCH DRINKS

Bairn

¾ oz. Scotch
½ oz. Triple Sec
1 dash orange bitters
Shake with ice. Strain over ice cubes.

Beadlestone

¾ oz. Scotch
½ oz. Dry Vermouth
Stir with ice. Strain into chilled cocktail glass.

Bobby Burns

¾ oz. Scotch
½ oz. Sweet Vermouth
2 dashes Benedictine
Stir with ice. Strain into chilled cocktail glass. Garnish with lemon peel.

Dry Rob Roy

1 ¼ oz. Scotch
¼ oz. Dry Vermouth
Pour over ice in a glass. Garnish with olive.

Godfather

¾ oz. Scotch
½ oz. Amaretto
Serve over ice.

Hoot Mon

¾ oz. Scotch
¼ oz. Littet Blanc
¼ oz. Sweet Vermouth
Combine all with cracked ice in a shaker. Shake well.

Strain into chilled cocktail glass.

Hop Scotch

1 oz. Scotch
¼ oz. Cointreau
2 dashes Orange Bitters
Fill highball glass with ice. Add and stir.

Mamie Taylor

1 ¼ oz. Scotch
Juice of ½ lime
6 oz. Ginger Ale
Pour scotch and lime over ice in a collins glass. Top with ginger ale and stir. Garnish with lemon peel.

Mint Sunrise

1 oz. Scotch
¼ oz. Brandy
¼ oz. Curaco
Stir gently with ice in a highball glass. Garnish with lemon slice and mint sprig

Perfect Rob Roy

1 oz. Scotch
¼ oz. Dry Vermouth
¼ oz. Sweet Vermouth
Serve in a glass over ice. Garnish with lemon twist.

Rusty Nail

1 ¼ oz. Scotch
¼ oz. Drambuie
Serve in a glass over ice.

Scotch Buck

1 ¼ oz. Scotch
½ oz. Lime juice
6 oz. Ginger Ale
Shake scotch and lime with ice. Strain over ice in a highball glass. Fill with ginger ale. Garnish with lime twist.

Scotch Cobbler

1 oz. Scotch
¼ oz. White Curaco
½ oz. Honey
Mix in a cocktail shaker. Shake well and drain into a chilled cocktail glass over ice. Garnish with mint sprig.

Scotch Rickey

1 ¼ oz. Scotch
Juice of ½ lime
6 oz. club soda
Pour scotch and lime into highball glass. Add soda and ice. Stir.

Scotch Sour

1 ¼ oz. Scotch
Juice of ½ lemon
½ tsp. Bar sugar
Shake with ice. Strain into chilled glass. Garnish with lemon slice.

Secret

1 oz. Scotch
¼ oz. White Crème de Menthe
Sparkling Water
Combine scotch and liqueur with cracked ice in a shaker. Shake well. Strain into chilled highball glass over ice and fill with water.

Stone Fence

1 ¼ oz. Scotch
1 dash Angostura bitters
Sparkling Apple Cider
Pour scotch and bitters into chilled highball glass over ice. Fill with cider and stir.

TEQUILA DRINKS

Anejo Banger

1 oz. Gold Tequila
6 oz. Orange Juice
¼ oz. Galliano
Blend tequila and juice with crushed ice. Pour over rocks and float galliano. Garnish with cherry.

Anejo Pacifico

1 ¼ oz. Tequila
½ oz. lime juice
½ oz. fruit syrup
Chill over rocks. Strain into cocktail glass. Garnish with lime slice.

Blue Meanie

¾ oz. Tequila
½ oz. Blue Curaco
2 oz. Sweet & Sour
Slat rim of cocktail glass. Shake well with crushed ice and strain into glass. Garnish with lime slice.

Brave Bull

¾ oz. Tequila
½ oz. Coffee Liqueur
Stir with ice. Strain into glass. Garnish with lemon peel.

Changuirongo

1 ¼ oz. Tequila
Ginger Ale
Pour into chilled collins glass filled with ice. Stir. Garnish with lime slice.

Margarita

1 oz. Tequila
¼ oz. Triple Sec

Juice of ½ lime
Shake with ice. Pour in salt rimmed margarita glass.

Matador

1 ¼ oz. Tequila
2 oz. Pineapple Juice
½ oz. lime juice
Shake with ice. Strain into glass. Garnish with lime slice.

Pinata

¾ oz. Tequila
½ oz. Crème de Banana
1½ oz. lime Juice
Shake with cracked ice. Strain into chilled cocktail glass.

T.L.C.

¾ oz. Tequila
Juice of ¼ lime
½ oz. Cognac
Shake well with ice. Strain into wine glass. Garnish with lime slice.

T.T.T.

1 oz. Tequila
¼ oz. Triple Sec
2 oz. Tonic
In wineglass mix tequila and triple sec with ice. Top with tonic and lime wedge.

Tequila Martini

¾ oz. Tequila
½ oz. Dry Vermouth
Stir with ice. Strain into cocktail glass. Garnish with olive.

Tequila Sour

1 ¼ oz. Tequila
Juice of ½ lemon
½ tsp. Bar sugar

Shake with ice. Strain into chilled sour glass. Garnish with lemon.

Tequila Sunrise

1 ¼ oz. Tequila
1 tsp. Grenadine
6 oz. Orange Juice
Pour Tequila and Grenadine over ice in a highball glass. Fill with orange juice and stir. Garnish with orange slice.

Tequini

1 oz. Tequila
¼ oz. Dry Vermouth
Stir with ice. Strain into chilled martini glass. Garnish with jalapeno pepper.

VODKA DRINKS

Bay Breeze

1 ¼ oz. Vodka
3 oz. Pineapple Juice
2 oz. Cranberry Juice
Combine in an ice-filled highball glass. Garnish with lime wedge.

Black Russian

¾ oz. Vodka
½ oz. Coffee Liqueur
Shake with ice. Strain over ice in a old-fashion glass.

Blue Lemonade

¾ oz. Vodka
½ oz. Blue Curaco
4 oz. Lemonade
Shake well and pour into

ice-filled collins glass. Garnish with lemon wedge.

Blue Shark

¾ oz. Vodka
½ oz. Tequila
3 dashes Blue Curaco
Combine in a shaker with ice. Shake well and strain into a chilled glass.

Bullfrog

1 ¼ oz. Vodka
1 tsp. Triple Sec
limeade
Pour vodka and triple sec over ice in a highball glass. Top off with limeade and stir. Garnish with lime wedge.

Cajun Martini

1 ¼ oz. Vodka
1 dash Dry Vermouth
Jalapeno Pepper
Combine vodka and vermouth in a mixing glass with ice and stir. Strain into a cocktail glass and drop in jalapeno.

Californian

1 ¼ oz. Vodka
3 oz. Orange Juice
3 oz. Grapefruit Juice
Combine in an ice-filled highball glass.

Cape Codder

1 ¼ oz. Vodka
6 oz. Cranberry Juice
Pour vodka over ice in a highball glass and fill with cranberry juice.

Blackberry Sip

¾ oz. Vodka
½ oz. Blackberry Brandy
2 oz. Sweet and Sour
Shake well with crushed ice. Strain into chilled cocktail glass. Garnish with lemon.

Copperhead

1 ¼ oz. Vodka
6 oz. Gingerale
Combine in an ice-filled collins glass.

Fashion Passion

1 ¼ oz. Vodka
2 oz. Grapefruit Juice
2 oz. Grape Juice
Shake well. Serve in an ice-filled collins glass. Garnish with two grapes.

Count Stroganoff

¾ oz. Vodka
¼ oz. Crème de Cocoa
¼ oz. Cointreau
Combine in a shaker with cracked ice. Shake well and strain into a chilled cocktail glass.

Greyhound

1 ¼ oz. Vodka
5 oz. Grapefruit Juice
Combine in an ice-filled highball glass.

Harvey Wallbanger

¾ oz. Vodka
6 oz. Orange Juice
½ oz. Galliano
Fill collins glass with ice. Add vodka and orange juice. Top with galliano.

Hawaiian Lemonade

1 ¼ oz. Vodka
4 oz. Lemonade
2 oz. Pineapple Juice
Combine in an ice-filled collins glass. Garnish with lemon twist.

Ice Pick

1 ¼ oz. Vodka
6 oz. Ice Tea
½ oz. lemon Juice
Combine in an ice-filled collins glass. Garnish with lemon wedge.

Kamikaze

¾ oz. Vodka
½ oz. Triple Sec
1 oz. Lime Juice
Shake and serve over ice in a large shot glass.

Kremlin Kernal

1 ¼ oz. Vodka
1 oz. Simple Syrup
½ oz. Water
Shake well with crushed ice. Strain into chilled cocktail glass. Garnish with mint leaves.

Licorice Slush

½ oz. Vodka
¾ oz. Anisette
1 scoop lemon sherbet
Blend until smooth. Pour in a highball glass. Garnish with licorice stick.

Melonball

¾ oz. Vodka
½ oz. melon Liqueur
2 oz. Orange Juice
Shake well with crushed

ice. Strain into cocktail glass.

Moscow Mule

1 ¼ oz. Vodka
Juice of 1.2 lime
6 oz. Ginger Ale
Pour vodka over ice in a highball glass. Squeeze lime over drink and drop in.

Mudslide

½ oz. Vodka
½ oz. Coffee Liqueur
¼ oz. Irish Cream Liqueur
Combine with cracked ice in a shaker. Shake well. Strain into chilled cocktail glass.

Orange Crusher

¾ oz. Vodka
½ oz. Triple Sec
2 oz. Orange Juice
Shake well with crushed ice and strain into cocktail glass.

Pineapple Lemonade

1 ¼ oz. Vodka
3 oz. Pineapple Juice
lemonade
Pour vodka and juice in a chilled collins glass over ice. Fill with lemonade and stir.

Pink Baby

1 oz. Vodka
¼ oz. Cherry Liqueur
2 oz. Sweet and Sour
Shake well with crushed ice and strain into cocktail glass.

Purple Passion

1 ¼ oz. Vodka
6 oz. Grape Juice
Pour vodka over ice in a highball glass. Fill with grape juice and stir.

Russian Rose

1 oz. Vodka
¼ oz. Grenadine
1 dash orange bitters
Combine in a shaker with cracked ice. Shake well and strain into chilled cocktail glass.

Salt Lick

1 ¼ oz. Vodka
2 oz. Lemon Soda
2 oz. Grapefruit Juice
Combine in an ice-filled wine glass with salt. Garnish with lemon wedge.

Salty Dog

1 ¼ oz. Vodka
6 oz. Grapefruit Juice
¼ tsp. Salt
Pour vodka over ice in a highball glass. Mix in salt and juice.

Screwdriver

1 ¼ oz. Vodka
6 oz. Orange Juice
Pour vodka over ice in a highball glass. Fill with orange juice.

Summer Sailor

¾ oz. Vodka
½ oz. Triple Sec
4 oz. Grapefruit Juice
Pour into ice filled collins glass.

Vodka Gimlet

1 ¼ oz. Vodka
½ oz. lime Juice
Shaker with cracked ice. Strain into chilled cocktail glass.

Vodka Martini

1 oz. Vodka
¼ oz. Dry Vermouth
Stir with ice. Strain into chilled cocktail glass.

Vodka Sour

1 ¼ oz. Vodka
Juice of ½ lemon
½ tsp. Bar sugar
Combine in a shaker with cracked ice. Shake well and strain into chilled sour glass. Garnish with lemon twist.

Vodka Stinger

¾ oz. Vodka
½ oz. Crème de Menthe
Shake well with crushed ice. Pour into ice-filled highball glass.

Vodka Tonic

1 ¼ oz. Vodka
6 oz. Tonic Water
Pour vodka over ice in a highball glass. Fill with water and garnish with lime wedge.

White Elephant

¾ oz. Vodka
½ oz. Crème de Cocoa
4 oz. half & Half
Combine in a ice-filled highball glass.

White Russian

¾ oz. Vodka
½ oz. Coffee Liqueur
2 oz. Heavy Cream
Combine vodka and liqueur in a glass over ice and fill with cream.

White Spider

1 oz. Vodka
¼ oz. Crème de Menthe
Stir with crushed ice and strain into chilled cocktail glass.

WHISKEY DRINKS

Apricot Sour

1 oz. Whiskey
¼ oz. Apricot Brandy
1 oz. Sweet and Sour
Shake well with crushed ice. Strain into a chilled sour glass.

Blackthorn

1 oz. Irish Whiskey
¼ oz. Dry Vermouth
1 dash Anisette
Stir well with crushed ice. Strain into a chilled cocktail glass. Garnish with lemon.

Boilermaker

1 ¼ oz. Whiskey
10 oz. Beer
Serve whiskey in a shot glass with a mug of beer.

Irish Cooler

1 ¼ oz. Irish Whiskey
1 ½ oz. Heavy Cream
Combine in an ice-filled Collins glass and stir.

Irish Delight

1 ¼ oz. Irish Whiskey
6 oz. Club Soda
Pour Whiskey in ice-filled
highball glass. Top with
soda and stir. Garnish with
lemon peel.

Manhattan

1 oz. Canadian Whiskey
¼ oz. Sweet Vermouth
Stir with ice in tumbler.
Strain into a chilled glass.
Garnish with cherry.

Salty John

1 ¼ oz. Whiskey
6 oz. Grapefruit Juice
Pour into salt-rimmed ice-
filled highball glass.

Snake Bite

¾ oz. Canadian Whiskey
½ oz. Peppermint
Schnapps
Shake well with crushed
ice. Strain into a chilled
pony glass.

Whiskey Sour

1 ¼ oz. Canadian
Whiskey
Juice of ½ lemon
½ tsp. Bar Sugar
Shake well with crushed
ice. Strain into a chilled
sour glass. Garnish with
lemon slice and cherry.

APPENDIX B: CIGARS

Cigar Names and Descriptions

Aliados—The Aliados hail from Honduras. It is a very spicy cigar with a medium bodied smoke. It has a hint of dried citrus and has rich flavors of coffee and spice. There is an earthy flavor on the palate.

Arturo Fuente—Fuente makes some of the most currently sought after cigars. They originate from the Dominican Republic. Their Opus X brand is one of the most coveted cigars you can smoke right now and is included in our big four of cigars (see above). The cigars are beautifully constructed and smoke exceptionally. The smoke has a hint of sweet spices.

Ashton—The Ashtons are created in the Dominican Republic. They are a well made cigar with a peppery smoke. The flavor is light and sweet. The finish is very earthy. The Ashtons smoke well from beginning to end.

Astral—The Astral cigars originate in Honduras. The cigars are smooth and have a nutty character to them. The smoke is usually mild and it has a woodsy finish.

Aurora—The Aurora is a product of the Dominican Republic. They have a very balanced flavor and are smooth tasting. There is a hint of sweet spice. This is a great after dinner cigar and is usually a terrific deal in the tobacco shops, where the cigar's suggested price is under $6.

Baccarat—The Baccarat is created in Honduras. It has a predominantly nutty flavor and is a medium bodied cigar. There is a hint of chestnut and other pleasant spices in the smoke. The finish has a decidedly coffee bean taste.

Bances—The Bances is from Honduras. It is a very smooth tasting cigar with a mild flavor. There is a distinct spice and cocoa flavor to the smoke. The finish is very strong. The smoke is consistent otherwise. The draw is even throughout.

Bauza—The Bauzas are created in the Dominican Republic and smoke with an earthly flavor. There is a kick at the end of the smoke, but generally it is a good cigar all the way through. The Bauza use Dominican Republic and Nicaraguan fillers, Mexican binders and Ecuadorian wrappers.

Bolivar—The Bolivars are created in both Cuba and the Dominican Republic. The Cuban Bolivars are legendary for their terrific smoke. The Dominican Republic cigars are terrific also, but do not compare to the Cuban version. These cigars are very solid and have a core of spiciness. They are very full bodied and are a decidedly smooth smoke. You cannot go wrong with a Bolivar.

Cacique—Cacique are created in the Dominican Republic. They are a medium bodied cigar with a very diverse taste. There are hints of coffee, orange, and hazelnut in the flavor, while maintaining a earthy overall taste.

Canaria D'oro—The Canaria D'Oro cigars are made in the Dominican Republic. These cigars are very smooth tasting, and are well-balanced. They have a creamy smoke with coffee bean and mild nut flavors. The finish is slightly spicy.

Cara Mia—Cara Mia originates from the Canary Islands. It is a medium bodied cigar with leather and coffee bean flavors. The finish is mild and the draw is consistent. The Cara Mias are a good choice in cigars.

Casa Blanca-—The Casa Blanca cigars are made in the Dominican Republic. They are smooth and medium bodied. There is a decidedly earthly flavor with notes of spice on the palate. These cigars get better with age.

Cascada—The Cascada cigars are made in Mexico. They are pleasant cigars although a little inconsistent. They have a hint of nut in the taste, and the finish is clean, fresh and mild.

V Centennial—The V Centennials are made in Honduras. There is a deep earthiness to this cigar. It has hints of orange peal with some toasty flavors. It has a good cedary finish while maintaining its consistency throughout.

Coaba—The Coaba are created in the Dominican Republic. These cigars have a sweet spice character with some leathery tastes on the palate. It is medium bodied and has a nutty finish. It is a consistent cigar.

Cohiba—One of the big four, the Cohiba originates from Cuba. If you can get a hold of a Cohiba you will not be disappointed. This cigar started out as Fidel Castro's personal cigar. They were made for him exclusively and given to foreign dignitaries that came by for meetings. Fidel has given up smoking, and the Cohibas are now available to the public. A terrific cigar in every aspect. The wrappers are beautiful, the flavor spicy and full, and the ash is strong and white. You can find some Cohiba marked Dominican Republic cigars which are created by a company that was smart enough to take advantage of the United States embargo on Cuban products and copyrighted the Cohiba name here in the U.S. The Dominican Cohibas are also very good and will be a terrific compliment to your collection.

Cruz Real—The Cruz Real is made in Mexico. It is a well made cigar with a firm draw and a very herbal character. There is a minty quality to the flavor.

Cuesta-Rey—The Cuesta-Rey is from the Dominican Republic. It is a cigar filled with sweet herbs with a hint of leather in the smoke. The cigar is well-balanced.

Cupido—The Cupido line is made in Nicaragua. These cigars are well-made with a smooth, leathery quality. The flavor hints of coffee beans and a pleasant cedar. The finish is mild and smooth.

Davidoff—Davidoff is created in the Dominican Republic. It is the cigar of choice for many of society's elite. The cigars are well-balanced and offer a light woodsy taste. There is a note of herbs on the palate and a touch of coffee on the finish.

Da Vinci—The Da Vinci is from Honduras. It is a pleasant, mild cigar. It is a creamy cigar with an earthy finish. There is a hint of spice flavors throughout the smoke.

Diplomaticos—The Diplomaticos originate in Cuba. Very rarely will you find a Cuban brand that is not consistently good, and the Diplomaticos are no exception. These are terrific cigars with a woodsy taste and smooth finish. They are full bodied and consistent throughout.

Don Asa—The Don Asa originates in Honduras. They have a nutty flavor with a slightly leathery finish. They have some rich spice notes on the palate. The draw is consistent.

Don Diego—Don Diego line originates in the Dominican Republic. It has some pleasing flavors of nuts and sweet wood. It is well made and has an herbal finish.

Don Leo-—The Don Leos are created in the Dominican Republic. They are a creamy cigar with a core of light herbs. The cigar is well balanced and leaves a light spice flavor on he palate.

Don Lino—Don Lino is made in Honduras. It is well-made and has a sweet character. The flavor hints of leather, nuts and cocoa bean. Overall it is a sweet cigar with a nice, consistent draw.

Don Mateo—The Don Mateo cigars are created in Honduras. They are a medium bodied cigar with a solid herbal character with some creaminess on the palate. There is a spicy and woodsy finish.

Don Ramos—Don Ramos is made in Honduras. They are well-made with a sweet tobacco component with a hint of cocoa. It has an overall creamy quality and a smooth even draw throughout.

Don Tomas—Don Tomas cigars are made in Honduras. This cigar is a well-balanced cigar. It is smooth and contains some herbal spices in the flavor. The finish is earthy and contains some leathery hints.

Don Xavier—The Don Xavier cigars originate in the Canary Islands.

This is a mild cigar. The flavor hints at wood and spices, and even some orange peel. The finish is decidedly woodsy and the draw is solid and consistent.

Dunhill—Dunhill cigars are made in the Dominican Republic. The Dunhill is a common choice among the upper crest of society. The cigars are superbly crafted and are terrific time and again. The cigars are mild and pleasant. The taste has a herbal creaminess and the finish has a hint of wood.

El Rey Del Mundo—The El Rey Del Mundo originate from both Cuba and Honduras. The Cuban version is a very strong cigar with a mix of spicy flavors. The Honduran version is a bit milder but still contains the spicy taste.

El Rico Habano—El Rico Habano is a product of the Dominican Republic. It is a mild to medium bodied cigar with a hint of toasty flavors. It has a very dry woody finish. The draw is very consistent throughout the smoke.

Escudo Cubano—The Escudo Cubano cigar is made in the Dominican Republic. It is a very solid cigar with a mild to medium body and some creamy flavors. There is a hint of burnt coffee and a very woody finish.

Fat Cat—The Fat Cat cigar is created in the Dominican Republic. It has a nutty taste with a strong woody quality on the finish. The smoke is medium bodied and the draw is consistent to the end.

Felipe Gregorio—Felipe Gregorio is a Honduran product. It is a mild to medium bodied cigar with a slight dry herbal character. The finish is woodsy and the taste is very smooth.

Flor De Florez—Flor De Florez is created in Nicaragua. This cigar has some very straightforward elements. There is a peppery taste, while being light and fresh. The finish hints at spice and the draw is excellent.

Flor De Gonzalez—Flor De Gonzalez hails from the United States, one of the few to do so. It is a solid smoke. There is a hint of cocoa bean in the smoke, along with a nutty and earthy finish. These cigars can be had for under $10 and are a good choice.

Fonseca—Fonseca is created in both Cuba and the Dominican Republic. The Cuban version is a very strong smoke full of flavor and character. The smoke is full of complicated spices and earthy flavors. The Dominican version is milder and a little more bland.

Garo—Garo cigars are created in the Dominican Republic. These cigars are terrific and come very highly rated from just about everyone who smokes them. The flavor is rich with spices and earthy tones. The draw is consistent and easy. The finish is woodsy. This cigar would be an excellent choice for any occasion and will impress anyone who tries it.

Gispert—The gispert is made in Cuba. This cigar has a nutty character. It is strong bodied with some spice on the palate and hints of wood on the finish. It is an easy draw and the cigar is consistent.

Griffin's—Griffin's originate in the Dominican Republic. It is a creamy cigar with a touch of coffee and a toastiness on the palate. The finish is fresh and clean with a hint of herbalness. The draw is consistent.

H. Upmann—H. Upmann is produced in both Cuba and the Dominican Republic. The H. Upmann is one of the more famous cigar lines being produced. The cigar is very well-balanced with a smooth and creamy character. There is a hint of leather and a cedary finish.

Habanica—the Habanica is created in Nicaragua. It has some subtle hints of spiciness. It is a medium-bodied cigar. It is straightforward and well-made. It has a slight touch of wood on the finish.

Habana Gold—This cigar from Honduras has a good looking wrapper. It is an elegant smoke with herb spices and earthy tobacco flavors. There is a hint of nut left on the palate. The cigar is a full-bodied smoke.

Havana Sunrise—The Havana Sunrise is produced in the United States. It is a full-bodied cigar with a strong earthy character. There is a hint of roasted nut on the palate. The finish has a touch of woodsy flavor.

Henry Clay—Henry Clay is made in the Dominican Republic. The Henry Clay is a pleasant, mild cigar. There is a hint of sweet spice in the taste. The wrapper is oily and pleasant. There is a touch of herb on the palate, and a woodsy finish.

Hoyo De Monterrey—The Hoyo De Monterrey is created in both Cuba and Honduras. This is a hugely popular brand of cigar right now, and rightfully so. The Cuban version is very strong and superbly crafted. The Honduran version is not far behind.

Both have a rich woodsy flavor with a touch of spice.

La Aurora—La Aurora originates in the Dominican Republic. It is a smooth, creamy cigar with a mild smoke. The finish is spicy and solid. The draw is consistent and easy throughout the smoke. This cigar is quite nice.

La Gianna—The La Gianna is a product of Honduras. It is a mild cigar with a pleasant spicy taste. The finish woodsy and dry.

La Gloria Cubana—La Gloria Cubana is made in both Cuba and the United States. These cigars are terrific. The United States version is probably the finest cigar created in America. The Cuban version is consistent and rich.

La Regenta—The La Regenta cigar is created in the Canary Islands. The cigar is rustic and has some good earthy tones. It has a sweet spice on the palate. The draw is consistent and easy from beginning to end.

La Tradicion Cabinet Series—La Tradicion is produced in the United States. It is a mild-bodied cigar with a some sweet spice and wood flavors on the palate. The finish is woodsy and the draw even and easy.

Lempira—The Lempira cigars are made in Honduras. This is an elegant cigar with a even draw. It has hazelnut and spice flavors, and a mild woody finish.

Macanudo—The Macanudo is created in Jamaica. It has built a solid reputation and is enjoyed by many cigar experts. The Macanudo has a beautiful oily sheen on the wrapper and has flavors of nuts and spice. It has a very earthy finish.

Maxius—Maxius is made in the Dominican Republic. It has a hint of cinnamon and nuts in its flavor. The finish is very woody.

Montecristo—One of the big four, the Montecristo is made in Cuba. The Montecristo is a beautifully made cigar. The flavor is very earthy and there are leather and woody hints. The finish is elegant and tasteful.

Montecruz—Montecruz is produced in the Dominican Republic. This is a medium-bodied cigar with a taste of orange and nut. The finish is woody.

Nat Sherman—The Nat Sherman is created in the Dominican Republic. It is a mild-bodied cigar with a smooth and spicy character. There are nuts and herbs in the flavor. The finish is woodsy and draw is even and consistent.

Olor—Olor is made in the Dominican Republic. It is a well-made cigar with a firm draw. It has an herbal quality with some spice on the palate. The finish is woodsy with a hint of spice.

Padron—The Padron cigar line is produced in Nicaragua. This cigar has a lot of character with some nutty and spicy flavors. The Padron is well-balanced and medium-bodied. The finish is earthy.

Partagas—Partagas brand originates from Cuba and the Dominican Republic. This is one of the most famous cigar brands available and is generally a terrific choice. The cigars in general have a huge amount of flavor, filled with spices and pepper flavors. Some cigars have a small amount of cocoa. In general, you cannot go wrong with a Partagas cigar.

Peterson—Peterson is made in the Dominican Republic. This cigar is mild-bodied with a smooth, creamy spice character. The flavor is spicy with some earthy hints.

Pleiades—The Pleiades is a product of the Dominican Republic. This is a spicy smoke. This cigar is medium-bodied with a fresh, clean quality. The flavor hints at nut and cedar, with an overall sweet taste.

Punch—Punch cigars originate from Cuba and Honduras. They are exceptional cigars with a terrific reputation. In general they are full bodied with a woodsy finish. The smoke is consistent and the draw is even throughout.

Regalos—One of the big four, the Regalos line is created in Honduras. This cigar is the top choice of many of today's major celebrities. There is no other word to describe a Regalos beside unbelievable. These cigars are superbly crafted and exquisitely made. Their taste is consistent cigar after cigar. Every cigar in the line is well-made and a terrific smoke. The maduro choices are unsurpassed. Another wise choice is the Presidente which is rich and even throughout its lengthy smoke. The Regalos cigars are rich-tasting and hint at mild spices from beginning to end. Begin your cigar experience with a Regalos and you might find you never have to try another brand. You cannot go wrong with a Regalos cigar.

Romeo Y Julieta—Romeo Y Julieta is produced in Cuba, Honduras and the Dominican Republic. The cigars range in quality. The Cuban versions are all very full-bodied and produce consistent quality smokes. The Dominican and Honduran versions are a little less consistent but generally very good. The Romeo Y Juleitas have a very good reputation.

Royal Jamaica—The Royal Jamaica cigar comes from the Dominican Republic. This cigar has a creamy spicy character with a earthy finish. This cigar is clean and has a very woody finish. The draw is even and firm.

Saint Luis Rey—The Saint Luis Rey is a Cuban cigar that is very strong. This full-bodied cigar offers mild spices in the flavor and hints of earthy tones. The finish is decidedly woody and the draw is even and consistent.

Sancho Panza—The Sancho Panza is produced in Cuba. This cigar is full-bodied and very strong. This cigar is consistent time and again, so if you like the first one you try, you are likely to like them all.

Servile—Servile cigars are made in the Dominican Republic. It is a mild, mellow smoke. There are hints of herbs and leather. The finish is woody and mild.

Sosa—The Sosa is created in the Dominican Republic. This is a well-made cigar with a very mild flavor. There is a hint of spice with a earthy component. The finish is also very mild. The draw is even.

Tamboril—The Tamboril is produced in the Dominican Republic. This cigar is a medium-bodied smoke with flavors that range in spices. There is a hint of cocoa and hazelnut. The finish is very woody.

Te-Amo—The Te-Amo is made in Mexico. The smoke is even and mild. The draw is firm and the flavor is subtle. The finish is strong.

Ultimate Dominican—The Ultimate Dominican is produced in the Dominican Republic. This cigar is an excellent smoke. I have heard many cigar smokers rave about this cigar. The look is elegant. The cigar is flavorful and tasty. The draw is even and easy.

Valdrych—Valdyrch is made in the Dominican Republic. The cigar is medium-bodied and has a pleasant character of wood. There is a touch of nuttiness on the palate. The finish is very woody and lengthy.

Vargas—The Vargas cigar line is created in the Canary Islands. This is a solid cigar with nutty, earthy tones. It has some sweet elements on the palate. The finish is subtle.

Zino—Zino is a product of Honduras. This is a well-made cigar. It is mild-bodied. There is a nutty taste. The finish if earthy.

Cigar Names and Countries of Origin

Aliados	Honduras
Arturo Fuente	Dominican Republic
Ashton	Dominican Republic
Astral	Honduras
Aurora	Dominican Republic
Baccarat	Honduras
Bances	Honduras
Bauza	Dominican Republic
Bolivar	Cuba, Dominican Republic
Cacique	Dominican Republic
Canaria D'oro	Dominican Republic
Cara Mia	Canary Islands
Casa Blanca	Dominican Republic
Cascada	Mexico
V Centennial	Honduras
Coaba	Dominican Republic
Cohiba	Cuba
Cruz Real	Mexico
Cuesta-Rey	Dominican Republic
Cupido	Nicaragua
Davidoff	Dominican Republic
Da Vinci	Honduras
Diplomaticos	Cuba
Don Asa	Honduras
Don Diego	Dominican Republic
Don Leo	Dominican Republic
Don Lino	Honduras
Don Mateo	Honduras
Don Ramos	Honduras
Don Tomas	Honduras
Don Xavier	Canary Islands
Dunhill	Dominican Republic
El Rey Del Mundo	Cuba, Honduras
El Rico Habano	Dominican Republic
Escudo Cubano	Dominican Republic
Fat Cat	Dominican Republic

Felipe Gregorio	Honduras
Flor De Florez	Nicaragua
Flor De Gonzalez	United States
Fonseca	Cuba, Dominican Republic
Garo	Dominican Republic
Gispert	Cuba
Griffin's	Dominican Republic
H. Upmann	Cuba, Dominican Republic
Habanica	Nicaragua
Habana Gold	Honduras
Havana Sunrise	United States
Henry Clay	Dominican Republic
Hoyo De Monterrey	Cuba, Honduras
La Aurora	Dominican Republic
La Gianna	Honduras
La Gloria Cubana	Cuba, United States
La Regenta	Canary Islands
La Tradicion Cabinet Series	United States
Lempira	Honduras
Macanudo	Jamaica
Maxius	Dominican Republic
Montecristo	Cuba
Montecruz	Dominican Republic
Nat Sherman	Dominican Republic
Olor	Dominican Republic
Padron	Nicaragua
Partagas	Cuba, Dominican Republic
Peterson	Dominican Republic
Pleiades	Dominican Republic
Punch	Cuba, Honduras
Regalos	Honduras
Romeo Y Julieta	Cuba, Honduras, and Dominican Republic
Royal Jamaica	Dominican Republic
Saint Luis Rey	Cuba
Sancho Panza	Cuba
Savinelli	Dominican Republic
Sosa	Dominican Republic
Tamboril	Dominican Republic

Te-Amo	Mexico
Ultimate Dominican	Dominican Republic
Valdrych	Dominican Republic
Vargas	Canary Islands
Zino	Honduras

ACKNOWLEDGMENTS

A special and sincere thank you to a few people who helped contribute to the making of this book: Earl Greenburg, Ian Shapolsky, Jill Bennett, Michele Hillion, Stephen Glassman and Craig Koller.

And now, the second annual presentation of the **Golden Wackerman Awards**—given to those people, places and things that gave us inspiration and support during this project: Bond "Jay" Bond, Robin, Ian, Earl, Meg, Craig, Adam, Leah, Laurie, Floyd, Jasmine, Amy, Colet, Bahman, Babak, Cydney Starpuck, Boomer Seymour (RIP), Jessie & Los Banos, Nicolle & all at Dance, Fuji-Miss-Moto, Teacher Maria, Steve-Nancy and a bucket of KFC, His & Hers (10-0), Campos (75), The Martins, Cindy, Lou & Heather, Woody Faircloth & all at Optel, Leah, Shaya & Scooter, Ms. "Rocko" Porter, Scott "Mr. ABQ" Porter, Brian "See Sucker" Foy, Teri & Terry, Charlie's Plumbing, David "Playboy" Condon, Doo Rag, The Goodwins, Starwagons, hurry with my free cigars, and make them good or I'll throw them out in front of you, Bug-DayDay-Chipper & Kram Grebhsrek, Al "Daily Scoop", Jodes-Stace-Rebecca B., Mrs. Javanbakht, Stacy & her Greek God Stelios, EROS Travel, Tsgt. William Ignacio Giavelli, Murray-Howard-Randy & all at Spectrum Products, Friar Allen, Glassman's Allen, Pierre and Yves, Lenny, Myron, Lynda, Rae, Scott,

Jeff and Joyce, Joel and Dana, Mike and Down Hillion, Carolyn and Roger, Tracy, John and Judy, Schwartzy and Shirley, Eugenie, Gigi, Franny, the great Las Vegas publicist Nana Ana and Max, Aunt Lil, Sadie and Sam, Lou, Jana, Mary, Richard, Tea, Megan, David, Kerry, Greg, Dusty, Kip, David and Zachary, Bob Dias & Jack Gallagher, Kevin Moda and Raffi, Dr. Hafarararar, Debbie and John, Dave and Spanky, Chelsey and JJ, Maty, Jim Borlaug, Ed Tabb, Gary Tabb, Rocky Perone, Alex & the fantasy league gang, Pure Platinum, the CyberSock, Denny Armstrong, Freaky Jason, super-babysitters Stephanie and Tiffany, LMB Incorporated, Elliot "The Human Party" Goldman and his lovely wife Heather Ann, Brother Mark, fuselage, ABS brakes, Mark of the law offices of Held, Held and Held (yes you can show causation for birth defects), Phill Swagel, Kristin Bauer, Evets Ettinger, Lena, Adam Carrola, Jimmy the Sports Guy, Kevin "Mr. Sports Advice" Fitzsimmons & my Sandbagger co-owner Mark Seban, Mertz, ASS, Llp., Don Knotts, Mike Giardina, Candy, Chris, Chris Jr., Nicole, Laurel, Larry Lee Rosnoski, Garry and Jenifer, Brian and Linda, Conan O'Brien, Rose—Rosario and Farshad, Menopause Manor, Richard Brustein, American Woman Magazine, Alva Motion Pictures, Jonathan Karsh, Vicky & Fred, Edward and all at Havanah Studios, Kevin at Geraldo, Rod/Elaine, John Woolard, Sir Edward-Lady Deb, Joe "DA BEARS" Shelfo, B.A.D. – Janie and all at DAC/BOEING, Danny & Sandy, Slugger Boy, D.J., Sandy (Petunia), Robert Redfeather, Cathy and Kyle, Jakey, Frank "Mr. La Brea and where's my lighter" McNeil, Father "That's enough out of you four" O'Brien, The Happy Bagel, Brickell, Derek Jeter (time for a toy), International Shoe, Shimm v. Bumpass, Crook & Chase, Swiss Boy and Lumpy, Capital Grill, Regalos, all at Loyola Law, Frank, Ana, Taufiki, Lawrence, Lewis—Mr. SkyBar, Dawn, Joel, Doug, John D'Sunopops, Prof. Goldman, Dean Levenson, Rose & Mike, my nut is getting out of hand, George and Athenian #3, Mandamus, Vin DiBona, John Goldhammer, Lloyd, Dom Irrera, Stuart Berton, Honey Almond, Gary Dell'Abate, Ronald Schaefer, Mad Dog and Micah, Fabio, the Lounge Baron, Lord of the Dance, the Count, the Traveler, Sweet Pea, Pez, MacInhoe, Clack, Paul Mitchell, Tarzan, Long Arms, Cell Phone Dude, Neil Armstrong, Wednesday, the Lumberjack, the Troll, No Hands, Blackletter, Mitten Man, Hark!, No Clothes, Eddie Murphy, George Jefferson, Barney Tardo, Band Aid Man, Morticia, Ellen DeBarones, Mrs. Spock, Martina, Trash Man, Johnny Mack, Nick's Cigars, everyone at CCH, Kim Dettwiller at Planet Hollywood, a special thanks to Elvis, and of course, most of all, Jill, Michele, Ryan, Kelsey, Brianne and Brittney.

Index

Other *Exciting* Titles from S.P.I. Books

Baseall Books You're Sure to Enjoy

- *A MUST-HAVE title for serious fans.*
- *The definitive Mantle book, documenting every homer in his career!*
- *Packed with 30 rare ACTION PHOTOS!*

MICKEY MANTLE'S GREATEST HITS: Dramatic Highlights of a Legendary Career
David S. Nuttall • $14.95 •1-56171-974-9

BOSTON RED SOX RECORDS by John A. Mercurio. Essential statistics, analysis and lore for Bosox fans. What rookie batting record of Ted Williams was broken by Fred Lynn in 1975? The last two no-hitters hurled by Red Sox pitchers came in the same season. Who pitched them? What fielding record does Hawk Harrelson share with Yaz? The answers to these questions—and all your questions about the Red Sox—are found in this book.
(ISBN: 1-56171-222-1) $4.99

N.Y. YANKEE RECORDS by John A. Mecurio. Essential statistics, analysis and lore for fans of the Bronx Bombers. Who held the Yankee record for most home runs in a season before Babe Ruth? Ron Guidry has struck out more men in a season than any other Yankee. Whose record did he beat? How many of the nine rookie records that Joe DiMaggio set have since been broken? The answers to these questions—and all your questions about the Yankees—are found in this book.
(ISBN: 1-56171-215-9) $4.99

THE BEST & WORST BASEBALL TEAMS OF ALL TIME by Harry Hollingsworth. Baseball's most amazing comparisons! Combining the savvy of a sports pro with the statistical magic of the computer. Nine decades of baseball's best & worst historical achievements are packed into this handy compendium of baseball facts & stats. Test yourself and friends on how much you REALLY know about baseball.
(ISBN: 1-56171-308-2) $5.50

Enjoy Life More With Self-Improvement Books

Hot Hollywood Titles from S.P.I. Books

Sweethearts of 60's TV The inspiring, heartwarming and surprising stories of the girls America tuned in to watch every week in the 60's. These glamorous and sexy stars made the 1960's a "time to remember" and long for, featuring Goldie Hawn and Judy Carne, Sally Field, Barbara Eden and more.
(ISBN 156171-206-X) $5.50 U.S.

Hollywood Raw by Joseph Bauer. Wouldn't you like to know how Christina Applegate and David Faustino (Kelly and Bud Bundy on *Married With Children*) live in real life? *Hollywood Raw* also includes informative sections on Kirstie Alley, Rosanna Arquette and Arsenio. Author Joseph Bauer was there on the sets as the studio teacher to the young stars. He saw first hand all the never-reported details of their shocking private lives.
(ISBN 1-56171-246-9) $5.50 U.S.

Hollywood's Unsolved Mysteries by John Austin. Here is the oddest collection of memorable stars of the big screen who have died in mysterious circumstances. From Marilyn, Natalie, and Bob Crane to William Holden, George Reeves and Vicki Morgan. Learn the truth behind the biggest cases!
(ISBN: 1-56171-065-2) $5.99 U.S.

Hollywood's Greatest Mysteries by John Austin. Hollywood columnist and author John Austin takes the reader well beyond the prepared and doctored statements of studio publicists to expose omissions and contradictions in police and coroner's reports. After examining these mysterious cases, you will agree that we have not been told the truth about Elvis Presley, Marilyn Monroe, Jean Harlow and others.
(ISBN 1-56171-258-2) $5.99 U.S.

The Latest In Good Health Info
for Smart Consumers

Perfect Lover: A Guide For Enhancing Everyone's Sex Life (and Dealing With Sexual Problems) by K.A. Hanash, MD. Here is clear and comprehensive advice about improving sexual performance for both young and old, male and female, and people with minor hang-ups or a major sexual dysfunction. The expertise and insights of both a urologist and psychologist help the reader meet both the physical and emotional needs of his/her partner.
(ISBN 1-56171-275-2) $5.99 U.S.

What Am I Eating? Facts Everyone Should Know About Foods by Dr. Mia Parsonnet. An all-purpose handbook designed to provide easy-to-understand, practical information about all the foods and vitamins we consume. Contains clear and concise answers to questions concerning food and nutrition, including: Are fast foods really so bad? Are health foods really so healthy? Is it wise to use bottled water? What is the record of vitamin supplements? Dr. Parsonnet has compiled an essential handbook for anyone concerned about their diet.
(ISBN 1-56171-034-2) $12.95 U.S.

Stop The Nonsense: Health Without the Fads by Dr. Ezra Soher. For everyone confused by the newest fads and "latest" discoveries about what's good for us and what's not, this book cuts through the clutter and delivers the straight facts. Dr. Sohar calls us to develop a logical, "life-style approach" to good health based on solid scientific evidence, reducing the confusion from the latest, often contradictory, medical advice.

   "... Offers a common sense approach to health and nutrition ... contrasts favorably with all the recently promulgated fads on dieting."-*Jean Mayer, President, Tufts University, Chairman (fmr), White House Conference on Nutrition and Health.*
(ISBN 1-56171-006-7) $11.95 U.S.